MURDER & MAYHEM
IN THE
WILLAMETTE VALLEY

MURDER & MAYHEM
IN THE
WILLAMETTE VALLEY

JENNIFER BYERS CHAMBERS

THE
History
PRESS

Published by The History Press
Charleston, SC
www.historypress.com

Cover images: Ghost town stagecoach, 2021. *Riley Chambers*; Oakridge, Oregon railroad tracks, near where the shootout to capture Ray Sutherland took place, 1942. *Russell Lee, Library of Congress, Prints and Photographs Division*; University of Oregon, Deady Hall. *Marion Dean Ross, Library of Congress Prints and Photographs Division*; booking photo of John Ackroyd, 1968. *From OregonLive/Oregonian*; policeman standing alongside wrecked car and cases of moonshine, 1922. *Library of Congress*; unidentified photo of men holding revolvers, 1910. *Oregon Records Management Solution*.

First published 2023

Manufactured in the United States

ISBN 9781467151740

Library of Congress Control Number: 2022949522

Notice: The information in this book is true and complete to the best of our knowledge. It is offered without guarantee on the part of the author or The History Press. The author and The History Press disclaim all liability in connection with the use of this book.

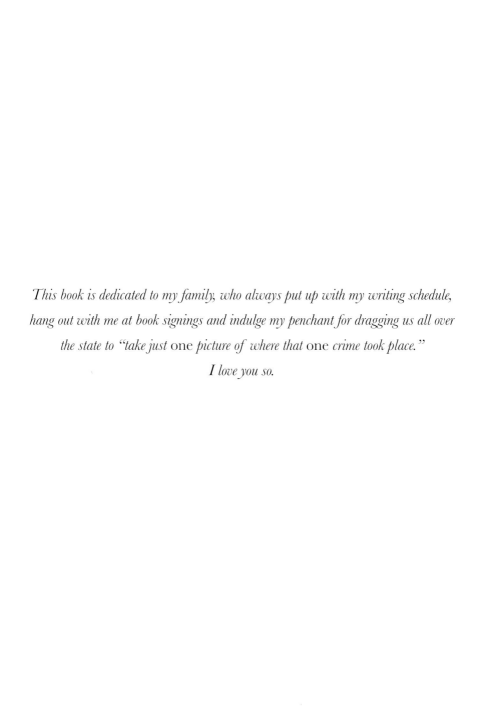

This book is dedicated to my family, who always put up with my writing schedule, hang out with me at book signings and indulge my penchant for dragging us all over the state to "take just one picture of where that one crime took place."

I love you so.

CONTENTS

PREFACE

I f you're reading this, you most likely share my own interest in true crime. The rest of my work, both fiction and non-, hasn't only been based in scary stuff. I have written horror several times, but most of my books are fiction; the nonfiction is historical and mainly women-centered. Finally, I made the time to catch up with my interest in true crime! I have lots more ideas in this vein. In between my historical research and writing, I like to go completely in the opposite direction. I'm endlessly interested in crime, cults and the unexplained. Too much *Twin Peaks*, *X-Files* and *Unsolved Mysteries* as a teenager maybe? Ah, the '90s.

Why is true crime a compelling subject? According to investigator Paul Holes in his 2022 book *Unmasked: My Life Solving America's Cold Cases*, there is a lot of interest in the subject, and for good reason. "The last number I heard was that four in every ten cases went unsolved," he wrote. "I counted at least six active serial killers in our country in the 1970s and '80s." Oregon, my home state, is the state with the "sixth greatest frequency of serial murders in the country," adjusted for population, according to the Federal Bureau of Investigation in an article on World Atlas. As we see in these pages, historical crimes are no different or less common than they are today…except, perhaps, that we know more about them. People do strange things. True crime is sometimes interesting because we can see ourselves in that situation. For example, many cults are expert at telling you what you want to hear so you'll join them. Other times, we read true crime to try to understand what could possibly draw a person to do such heinous things. Nothing is as scary as real life.

My simple goals for writing about true crime and other nonfiction are based loosely on similar rules from author Paul Holes, paraphrased here:

- Have empathy for the people involved in the cases, but also curiosity and an open mind. Yes, by and large these are unexplainable acts. By understanding the period or extenuating circumstances, we can at least put ourselves in the time and place, if not gain a greater understanding of the context of the worlds these events occurred in.
- Have compassion for the victims and try to have the same for the perpetrator as much as I am able. These are real people, no matter the period their stories take place. Real families. True stories. I try not to sensationalize whenever possible to keep that in the forefront of my mind. Sometimes, I must go into more detail than I'd like, but that's true crime.

Here's my own addition: Be kind and curious. Whether they are moonshiners or pioneers or cult leaders, the characters in these pages are operating the best way they can, no matter if you and I understand it or not.

What makes these people different than regular Joes with hopes, dreams, families and needs? What is broken? Is it nature or nurture? Is it driven by love or desperation, or are some people just evil? What do those who perpetrate heinous acts do when faced by these things or events, and what makes us make different choices?

ACKNOWLEDGEMENTS

My thanks to the researchers and librarians who helped me with this book. I'd like to single out the Oregon State University and University of Oregon librarians and particularly the fine facility and staff at the Fern Ridge Public Library, who are unfailingly kind and helpful. Thank you to Noelle Crombie, whose fine reporting led me to the story of Rachanda Pickle and the "Ghosts of Highway 20" series (watch it, it's chilling) and down the rabbit hole to find out more. Huge thanks to Jason Chambers, Riley Chambers, Pat Edwards and Marna Hing, who provided personal photos for the book.

NIMROD O'KELLEY

TRESPASSING ON MURDER

The early Oregon Trail was traversed by more than 500,000 people from the 1840s to the 1870s. It led a long and arduous path to the fertile, green valley and dark trees that made up the land of the West, and wagon ruts still line some of those trails today. Many of these travelers ended up in the nearly thirty-mile-wide-by-one-hundred-mile-long corridor of the Willamette Valley that now roughly travels the main highway Interstate 5, or the "I-5." As we will see in later chapters, the history of violence did not stop with the skirmishes with natives over the settlers' idea of Manifest Destiny as the largely white settlers made their way into the West Coast. Unfortunately, many of those anti-native acts were not recorded. The colonizers did not hesitate to report the often-brutal violence against one another.

The first provisional American government, a way to lasso the lawless and give structure to the settlement, was started in Salem, Oregon, in 1843. The Oregon Donation Land Claim Act, in 1850, gave a white man the right to claim 320 acres, or half a square mile, of land on his own, and they could appropriate one full mile, or 640 acres of land, on behalf of himself and his wife. This act passed before any treaties were made with native tribes of the area, and according to the State of Oregon, "Only 'white settlers' and 'American half-breed Indians' could claim land, and the Act excluded all non-U.S. citizens, including Native peoples, who were not considered by law as U.S. citizens at the time, Blacks, and Hawaiians." The makeup of the Oregon Territory was still a question for the people of what was then considered the "West." The westernmost part of the states was then

The Covered Wagon, sculpture by Leo Friedlander, 1934; photographed between 1980 and 2006. *Carol Highsmith, Photographs in the Carol M. Highsmith Archive, Library of Congress, Prints and Photographs Division.*

considered to be Iowa or possibly Missouri, depending on who you asked. President James Polk, freshly elected in 1844, received a lot of grief from all the different groups of people who wanted to move to Oregon territory, as well as those who would just have soon kept the borders where they were.

Into this environment came Nimrod O'Kelley. He was born in Tennessee in 1780. Records show him in the military as of 1812, when he was twenty-two. He and his wife, Sarah or "Sally" Bell, were married in Tennessee in 1813. Together, they are recorded as having ten children between 1813 and 1841. Such a quantity of children was not unusual. According to the U.S. Census, families averaged six to nine children in 1850.

He had traveled on the Oregon Trail in 1845, at age sixty-five, on the tail end of those who were chasing gold. O'Kelley had enjoyed a full life before he even started the journey. The single men often joined a wagon train of others and banded together in larger groups for safety. A single person was advised to have a large but sturdy wagon, two hundred pounds of flour, one hundred pounds of bacon and a large quantity of pilot biscuits

Stained-glass window showing pioneers as a nineteenth-century family around a Conestoga wagon on the prairie, 1857. *Library of Congress.*

or hardtack for when cooking material was not plentiful. Most people drove all the oxen they could afford attached to their team. The road was littered with possessions that had been discarded from multitudes of passing wagons. The weather was horrendous. It was blazing sun, torrential rain and long days but beautiful sunrises and sunsets according to Oregon Trail Diaries. Rainstorms and raging rivers took out oxen and people routinely, and there were more ways to die than they could have ever known. Still, nearly three thousand migrants made it to the territory in 1845. The movement almost doubled the number of those in the native tribes who lived there.

We can assume that O'Kelley faced much the same circumstances, although we do know that he was not in the group of wagons that took the ill-fated Meek Cutoff; it was the first wagon train to the territory in 1845, where many perished and many others were forced to turn back and take another arduous route due to frontiersman leader Stephen Meek's poor directions. There are no records that survive from O'Kelley's overland passage, other than he crossed in 1845 and signed some records at a fort at that time. While it may have been the end of the time of those who searched for gold, the quest for fertile land was still on.

The land was covered in six-foot-tall grasses and first-generation (what we now call "old growth") Douglas fir, ponderosa pine, madrone and oak trees. Much of the valley was wetlands. These are what make the land valuable, in addition to the loamy soil and abundant crops. The settlers quickly made the area their own, as Kay Atwood and Dennis J. Gray wrote for the Oregon History Project:

> With settlement, the land changed forever. White farmers turned Native village sites and camas fields into pastures and converted native grasses to wheat and oats. Within months, Di'tani became Table Rock, Me-tus became Humbug Mountain, and Dilomi became Jacksonville. The Euro-Americans gave new names to the creeks and mountains, calling them Wagner Creek, Sexton Mountain, and Hunter Creek.

Upon arrival, O'Kelley claimed his one square mile (or 640 square acres) as settlers were promised, holding half of that amount in his wife's stead. His family was "coming soon," he said. His claim that his wife was coming on a future migration was believed in the short term, but by 1852, he still had no wife present in Oregon country to back up his claim. Letters from home indicate that she was waiting with the kids while the sale of a property was determined, as well as to give him the chance to make their claim.

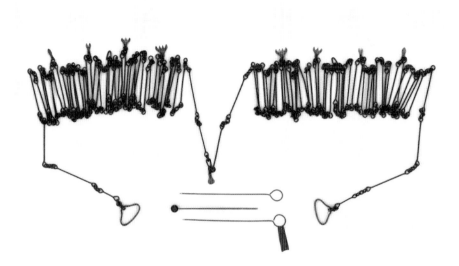

Gunter's Chain. A twenty-two-yard or sixty-six-foot-long chain, used to measure one acre, 1800. *Library of Congress.*

Reports from neighbors are mixed. Some say that he arrived alone and set up his property on his and his wife's share and a half of land, the extra half being a benefit from being a war veteran. They wrote that he kept to himself. Most accounts paint him as a brusque man, a man not overly concerned with the opinions of his neighbors, yet he proved to have a strong, if confusing, sense of morality.

O'Kelley was, according to author Ronald Lansing in his book *Nimrod: Courts, Claims and Killing on the Oregon Frontier,* connected to America in many symbolic ways. When he was born, the Revolutionary War was on, and he was three years old when it ended. He was surely old enough at twenty-six, as Lansing stated, to remember the tales of Lewis and Clark when they returned from their trek west. Perhaps that was part of what fueled his desire to explore.

O'Kelley has been described as a devoted Roman Catholic. Some sources say that he was at one point planning to become a priest and was educated at a Catholic college, all the way up to learning multiple languages. It is agreed that he was dedicated to his faith to the point of bigotry. He was vehemently Catholic, "zealous" and "infatuated in his religious belief." Religious strife was high at that time in the area, with anti-Catholic rhetoric, and plainspoken O'Kelley may not have endeared himself and his claim with locals, who populated the area with mainly "hardcore anti-Catholic Protestants."

The letters that O'Kelley sent his wife about his property, inviting the family to come join him, took a long time to get there. Part of that was probably the unreliable overland mail system. However, there isn't a satisfactory answer as to why his wife took so long to join him. It's tempting to infer that his temper was hot, given this story, and that they may have preferred to live apart, but there isn't any evidence to support that theory other than the incident that follows. After he set up his homestead, Jeremiah Mahoney disputed his claim to the land because he did not believe that O'Kelley had a wife at all. He squatted on the property farthest from O'Kelley's cabin, set up tents and claimed it for his own. Mahoney filed an official counterclaim for the acreage and moved his own family there.

The irony to all of this is that the land that the two men squabbled over was within the original territory of the Kalapuya tribe. The area had been devastated and the tribes decimated by smallpox and malaria outbreaks upon settlement by Europeans in the early 1800s, leaving the land vulnerable to colonization and the creation of "plats" by settlers in the first place.

The two men had verbal spats every time they met. Eventually, O'Kelley carried a shotgun with him wherever he walked. On May 13, 1852, O'Kelley was walking along his fence line near his barn when he saw a man approaching. The man, Mahoney, was reported in some sources to be armed. He was known to pace his property holding a rifle.

A handmade knife with antler handle, by Ron Bjerklund, made and photographed in 2022. *Jason Chambers.*

T.B. Odeneal, reporting from the *Oregonian* newspaper, said that "[a]t this time, when land was so abundant, it is not easy to excuse a man for setting up any doubtful claim over which he might waste years and lose the chance to secure a good donation."

On May 13, the arguments with Mahoney escalated to the breaking point. O'Kelley walked over, calmly and methodically, and "filled him full of buckshot." After Mahoney's death, O'Kelley reportedly took care of the body and then, seemingly equally as placidly, walked to Marysville, or what is now Corvallis, to turn himself in to the authorities there.

That's where the story gets even stranger. By that evening, Mahoney's wife had grown increasingly more worried when he did not return. When he was found dead, his wife and friends organized a search party to find O'Kelley and bring him to justice.

Oddly, a man showed up at the crime scene and said that he was the justice of the peace. The trail of people involved in this story is made from people seemingly arbitrarily appointed to various positions of authority in the case. The hunt for O'Kelley began quickly and search parties were made of neighbors and townspeople, but they could find neither hide nor hair of the man. O'Kelley was already on his way there on his own. He had walked all the way to the courthouse in Marysville.

O'Kelley maintained that Mahoney accosted him and wanted to know why he was armed. Mahoney then tried to grab the gun and hit him over the head. The gun went off, O'Kelley said by accident, in the struggle that ensued. His complete statement about the incident, according to a declaration filed on June 3, 1852, read:

The Declaration of Nimrod O'Kelley
This Irishman has been an intruder on my land or claim for two or three months. I was not afraid of his holding claim but he would threaten him every time I would meet him on my own claim. On the twenty-first of this month I started out around my field where I was expecting to find some crows intruding on my farm when I met this Irishman or came within a few steps of him but neither of us spoke as I had told him to keep off my claim he did not speak to me. I went home and got my horse and went to the field to plowing & continued to work until dinner time of day, after which I started he met me again near my house coming towards my house. When about ten steps apart he asked me why I was always carrying my gun for. I remarked to him it was none of my business it was my own. He continued coming towards me saying if I did not mind I would get it threshed out over my head. I made no reply for a short (time) but told him to stand off and got out of the path he got off the path also, rather sidling up towards me in a stopped position before however before getting near enough to me to get ahold of the gun the gun went off in my hands hitting him I know not where I have no recollection of ever cocking the gun but held her down at arms length. I saw him set down I left immediately after traveling some distance I saw him lay down I came to town directly to give myself up to the proper officer, where I make this declaration.
Written by A.I. Babb.

The victor writes the history, though, so who knows what the truth really is?

The authorities issued a warrant for murder the day he was brought in. The trial, the first murder trial in the Oregon Territory, began in June. Although his defense lawyer, A.J. Babb, cited no fewer than nine proven errors in the trial, O'Kelley's trial ended in a verdict of guilty, and he was sentenced to the gallows. His death was to occur a month from the time of the trial. In the meantime, his attorney brought claims of wrongdoing to the Oregon Supreme Court. One of these was improper jury selection, which was germane given the religious makeup and feuds of his peers. Despite that and other improprieties, his conviction was upheld. It is notable that people in multiple communities in the area protested his sentence and instead added support to O'Kelley's case. The bottom line in this trial was that the judicial system was not yet capable of carrying out the proceedings correctly. Add to that the fact that the only evidence was given by O'Kelley himself—altogether an issue not too easily solved.

In Oregon Territory, committing murder was a crime punishable by death. Not so in other colonies, where the original charge of murder could be argued against if the accused could ask for the "plea of benefit of clergy," that is, a way for clergymen to get out of a death penalty by being able to

Ghost town stagecoach, 2021. *Riley Chambers.*

read the first verse of Psalm 51. Another way used for getting out from under the death penalty was through "wages of battle," an antiquated way for the accused to battle the accuser to decide his fate. The third method that called for the death penalty in early America was "petit treason" or the killing of a master by his slave, a husband by a wife and so on, and these cases were death by hanging (men) or burning at the stake (women). Not so in Oregon. Murder generally called for the death penalty in return.

One version of what happens next in this case is the version that seems the most plausible. O'Kelley spent forty days and nights in the jail. He was then sent home to wait for the execution, with a stern warning to be there promptly at the hour he was due. The execution, which was supposed to be June 9, 1854, never happened. Sarah O'Kelley had finally gotten those letters. She was on the way. One of their sons took a horse and rode to prove their existence to the Benton County authorities. He made it at the absolute last hour, after O'Kelley had returned to the holding cell, and said that his mother was on her way. Sheriff T.J. Right let O'Kelley out of the jail cell immediately and trusted the courts to catch up.

The "woman riding in a on a white horse to save the day" trope would be unfortunately disproven. Documentation shows that Governor John Pollard Gaines canceled the first execution. The second ruling on the appeal by the Oregon Supreme Court was curious. The court admitted that several things about the previous trial were incorrect. The grand jurors weren't required to be sworn in and weren't even examined for whether they were qualified. When they read the verdict, it wasn't "rendered in open court, nor in the presence of the defendant. Apparently, the jury just sent word to the judge that the guy was guilty and went home," as Finn J.D. John has noted. O'Kelley went home, too, and was permitted to live with his family, who had arrived while he was in jail, until further notice. All of them were living on the property by now and, by all accounts, built up their farm and land together.

His third sentence was canceled by Governor John Wesley Davis a scant five minutes before the sentence was to be carried out. It was instead converted to two years in prison. As he had walked to the Marysville government to turn himself in when the crime was first committed, O'Kelley transported himself voluntarily. After the wagon the sheriff had hired to bring him to the penitentiary broke down, he walked right to the hotel the wagon had intended to get to. After waiting there for a time, the wagon never showed up, so O'Kelley turned himself in to the prison superintendent. The man simply did not believe his crazy story and sent

Abandoned pioneer cabin, 2021. *Riley Chambers.*

him away. Eventually, the sheriff and his wagon got to the jail, and he was retrieved and committed to the Oregon State Penitentiary to serve his sentence. This verdict was recorded as the Oregon Supreme Court's first murder conviction in the state. A son came to visit O'Kelley often and sat outside his cell. He was by that time seventy-four years old.

This sentence was cut short, however. Governor George Law Curry gave him a pardon in August 1855 for good behavior. When O'Kelley returned home, he found that Mrs. Mahoney and her children were still living on the back half of his claim. Abruptly, he decided to set out to take his case all the way to the U.S. General Land Office. Off he went to Washington, D.C., on train, horseback and mainly on foot, thousands of miles back over the Oregon Trail. He did this at seventy-five years old.

His aim was to turn his original claim of land to a new land patent and hoped to get some sympathy by right of his time in the service, but he was unsuccessful. He died of old age in 1864. His land claim was still unclear. Eventually, O'Kelley, along with his wife, Sarah, were posthumously given the rights to the full mile of land in 1881. Upon his death, his half of the land went to the Catholic Church. His wife did the same with her half of land when she passed.

Scotts Bluff and the Oregon Trail, 1941. *Marion Post Wolcott, Farm Security Administration— Office of War Information Photograph Collection, Library of Congress.*

One of the stories told about the town of Nimrod's name origin is about an inn and a town called Nimrod possibly named after O'Kelley. Nimrod of the Bible was a king and a successful hunter, so according to the area's website, that might be the reason for the name, but there is no proclamation either way. He had been a lifelong fisherman and invented a self-named and patented fishing lure at some point in his life, so it's possible. Either way, the tale of Nimrod O'Kelley makes for a good story for the name of the fishing town on the banks of the McKenzie River.

CHARITY LAMB

THE HUSBAND AND THE HATCHET

The stories about Charity Lamb in the *Oregonian*, *Oregon Spectator* and *Oregon Weekly Times* are as lurid as you might expect from a tabloid of today. "Murderess" and "A Monster," they cried. "Think of it, ladies! If any of you feel disposed to walk up behind your husbands or fathers and chop their heads open, why, just pitch in—you are safe in doing so!" One modern article about her contends that "unlike her name, she was neither charitable or a lamb."

On the evening of May 13, 1854, as the family were being entertained by her husband Nathaniel Lamb's story of bear hunting around the table, Charity Lamb silently picked up an axe from the woodpile outside and brought it down onto the back of his head. The blow was hard enough to force her to heave it out because it was stuck. Then she hit him again. After she made the blows to her husband's head, Lamb dropped the axe and ran out the back door. Her story makes her the first woman convicted of murder in the Pacific Northwest. It was also one of the first times that self-defense as a tactic was used as the impetus for murder.

One account says that her husband was able to walk around afterward. Another view asserts that he fell immediately from the table onto the floor. He did not perish until a week later, however. Charity was found later at a neighbor's home about a half mile away, smoking a cigar and cowering from her husband in hopes that he had not chased after her.

The papers were relentless and called the act "cold blooded and atrocious," a "revolting murder." Their sons Abram, who was thirteen at the time, and

Tomas, who was nine, were reportedly sitting at the table when the act occurred and testified to that effect at her trial. Their daughter, Mary Ann, who was nineteen, was either sitting in the room or sitting in the adjoining room. Their newborn baby, Presley, was lying in a cradle somewhere in the house.

Later, Charity would say that she "did not mean to kill the critter...only intended to stun him" and conversely that "she was sorry she had not struck him a little harder." It would transpire to become what we would see now as a clear case of spousal abuse leading up to an impossible situation for the victim. She has even been called "Oregon's Lizzie Borden."

Although she may have been mentally ill, according to modern standards, as well as being a victim of spousal abuse, she was conceivably not at times a very good person. The *Oregon Statesman* reported in 1889 that she was a "she-devil" who didn't garner much sympathy: "After she was

The Pioneer, University of Oregon. The statue, praised by the Oregon Historical Society president at the time as an Anglo-Saxon monument to assimilation, has since been removed. *Oregon Historical Society (publisher), Alexander Phimister Proctor (sculptor), 1919.*

committed to the Penitentiary, she was put to work in the kitchen, but she was detected mixing ground glass into the victuals for condiments, so she was transferred to the [Hawthorne] Asylum."

To be fair, Charity was worn out. The near forty-year-old had lived a tough life before that point, and now she had a much tougher one in rural Oregon. The Lamb family cabin was not large. It sat among rough land with "second and third rate" soil and a "soot-covered ceiling." It was one of nine such cabins in the areas adjoining the Clackamas River, and the nearest of these was far away, certainly out of earshot, as the parcels each claimed were 318 acres.

The couple had met and married where they lived in North Carolina in 1837. Although it is unknown where Charity was born, she may have been from North Carolina or northern Virginia originally. Apparently, and rather unusually, she had learned to read and write either in her home or at school. Their first child, Mary Ann, was born to the farmer and his wife less than a

Left: Pioneers, from the book *Woman Triumphant*, 1919. *Rudolph Cronau.*

Opposite: Old axe in a stump, 2013. *Sergio Magpie.*

year later. At one point, they moved on to Indiana. The U.S. Census has the family, now with four kids, in White, Missouri, by 1850. Indeed, they were pioneers the whole of their married lives.

They traveled the Oregon Trail to the Clackamas area, near Oregon City, still known as the "End of the Oregon Trail," the first incorporated city that lay west of the Mississippi River. It was considered the edge of the wilderness, and the Lamb family set their land hopes on the outskirts of town and applied for the full-measure land patent there. The area was the site of a large tragedy shortly after they arrived. The *Gazelle*, a sternwheeler steamboat on the Clackamas River, exploded due to a boiler problem, and twenty-five people were killed, while another thirty were injured. It was

the biggest such accident ever to happen in the Northwest up to that point and was a blow to the small town, which supported the steamboat and lumber industry with labor and fabrication. The Lambs built their home adjacent to, but not precisely nearby, other settlers and attempted to raise their children and build a new life there.

Their marriage was never a happy one. Nathaniel had a problem with alcohol and threatened his family with violence if they revealed that he had stolen livestock. Charity grew more and more frail, particularly after 1853, when her fifth child was born. During her trial, Charity would testify that Nathaniel tried to poison her and that during their overland trip, she carried his gun at the front of their wagon train so that he would not use it against her, as he had threatened. According to later testimony by their children, Nathaniel regularly beat Charity for little reason. Her "infractions" were as small as refusing to help carry a log. According to author Finn J.D. John, in 1853, when the log incident occurred, Charity was likely pregnant. Two other major episodes occurred that year: Nathaniel hit Charity by throwing a hammer at her head, and he threatened to shoot her when she attempted to leave him. Sometime in the winter before Nathaniel was killed, "he knocked her down with his fists and kicked her over several times in the snow."

The family met a man who stayed at a neighboring farm in 1853. With so few residents, a new face may have been exciting; for Mary Ann especially, a new face brought the possibility of a new life elsewhere. Mr. Collins was staying there in exchange for some work and had since moved on to California. Neighborhood gossip had it that Mr. Collins attempted to seduce both Charity and nineteen-year-old Mary Ann, with whom Collins communicated via letter. One of the newspapers alleged that either Mary Ann or Charity, writing on Mary Ann's behalf, had received a letter from Collins at some time shortly before the murder and that Nathaniel had found it after it had been hidden either in the home or on Charity's person, giving a likely motive for the crime.

The *Oregon Weekly Times* alleged that Charity and Mary Ann had planned to have Mary Ann elope with Mr. Collins and that Nathaniel's seizure of the letter from him in the week before the crime was the perfect motive for the murder. That week, Nathaniel told Charity multiple times that he was going to kill her and abandon the rest of the family so that he could move to California. He even said he was going to wait until the pregnant cow had delivered her calf so he could leave Charity and take the baby with the children and himself to start a new life there without the bother of the nursing mother. He was quoted as having said that she "would not live on his expense longer than a week; that he was going to kill her next Saturday night."

The letter made it all worse. Abram Lamb, their thirteen-year-old son, testified that his father told his mother the morning of the bear hunt that if she thought about leaving that day, he would find her and "settle her when she didn't know it" and that "I heard her say that morning, before I went out with Pap hunting, that he was going to kill her, and she didn't know what to do." Anne Jennings Paris wrote in a poem about Charity the morning of the murder:

> "Kill your woman later," I hear our neighbor yell.
> "We got a bear to hunt." They laugh, and I'm spared.

The next threat that occurred was even more chilling. Nathaniel and Charity were by themselves for a moment in the yard as Abram and the neighbor prepared for their hunt. Nathaniel may have thought they were alone, but Abram saw his father as he steadied his gun on the railing and aimed the rifle at Charity. Nine-year-old Thomas Lamb testified that he saw it too and that only when Mary Ann turned toward them did his father turn his sights off Charity and aim the shot at a tree.

It is not known what Charity did while the men were off hunting. It is easy to assume that she went about the regular, arduous business of the pioneer woman, scrubbing, laundry, nursing the baby, preparing food from scratch, gardening and more. The weather would have been seasonally wet and muddy. May is humid and rains an average of 20.3 days over the month, so even if it was a non-rainy day, the ground would likely have been wet; no clothing or bedding would ever feel truly dry. It's also easy to imagine that perhaps she spent the day plotting her revenge. This crime may have been justified in her eyes, but it seems as if Charity just saw opportunity and took it rather than plan a complicated murder scheme. She was certainly mistreated on a regular basis. It may have been routine at the time, but it's hard to imagine today taking on that amount of work and that kind of abuse for what amounted to indentured servitude with no exit date.

For whatever reason, Charity chose the dinner table when Nathaniel was busy eating and bragging to the family about his hunting prowess as the right

Ox team pioneer Ezra Meeker (1830–1928) went over the Oregon Trail in 1852. This is a drawing of his first cabin. *From* Ox-Team Days on the Oregon Trail *(1922).*

time. Her testimony seems honest—that she only meant to stun him rather than kill him, and as horrible as it sounds, the stunning at least does sound almost understandable to modern ears.

Immediately after the crime, the children's eyewitness testimony stated that Nathaniel, with the axe buried a few inches into his skull, fell to the ground and did not die right away. "He fell over and scrambled about a little," Abram said.

Charity ran out of the room upon hitting Nathaniel and dropped the axe in the yard. She spent the night at the neighbors until the authorities found her the next day. I have not seen a firsthand account of what the children did during this time. A doctor must have been called because it is recorded that Dr. Presley Welch monitored Nathaniel, who was "screaming and covered with blood," although he eventually died a few days later, probably of infection. Nathaniel did give several statements that implicated and impugned Charity before he passed away.

On September 11, 1854, the trial began. It was held with an all-male jury. The makeup was hardly a jury of her peers, but women were unable to serve on juries in Oregon until 1912. Charity—who had grown ever more sickly and was described as "emaciated and sallow" and wearing dirty, threadbare clothing—was represented by defense lawyer James Kelly. The defense he mounted centered on Charity being not guilty by reason of insanity, a "monomaniac," or one obsessed or preoccupied with one idea or thing. The defense argued firstly that she could not have been in her right or rational mind when the crime occurred and that, secondly, she was afraid for her own life.

The prosecution called an expert medical witness who countered that she was "very much excited…looked wild-like out of her eyes," and that he "thought she was pretending." Furthermore, Charity had implicated herself when she ran from the scene of the crime. She showed premeditation in her choice of weapon. Also, she had not seemed remorseful when authorities found her. Instead, she was calmly smoking a cigar at the neighbor's home.

The jury had a hard time deciding on her guilt or innocence. They had been meeting for half a day before they returned to ask the judge questions. What entails "imminent danger"? And what is justifiable self-defense?

While there was no dispute that she killed him, she did so out of fear of her own life, her lawyer had argued. Judge Cyrus Olney told the jurors to determine whether Charity "acted out of a genuine belief in self-preservation" when they made their decision. In other words, was she in *immediate* danger? "If she saw danger," said Olney, "it was her duty to have gone away."

They decided quickly after that. Their verdict read, "Charity Lamb is guilty of the killing purposely and maliciously…but without…premeditation and do recommend her to the mercy of the Court." She was convicted of second-degree murder, the sentence that Olney thought was as lenient as the law would allow. She was not allowed to testify in her own defense but was given the chance to speak for the first time at sentencing:

> *Well, I don't know that I murdered him. He was alive when I saw him last.…I knew he was going to kill me.…He told me not to go, and if I went that he would follow me, and find me somewhere, and he was a mighty good shot.…I did it to save my life.*

Imagine the scene: a skeletal woman holding an infant, milk staining the rags she wore, as the baby was wrested from her arms. Charity spent two years in the Oregon City Jail and then was transferred to the Portland Penitentiary to become convict no. 8. Her work there started as heavy labor. In her case, heavy labor meant work in the prison laundry, where her work included scrubbing and mangling (wringing out in a manual machine) the sheets and clothing of everyone from the orderlies and directors to the inmates. She worked diligently and was given a commendation or award for her "hardiness" in the prison newspaper. Although all other males in the prison who had the same sentence of second-degree murder were released after two years, she was never let go, either through clerical error or otherwise.

She grew increasingly erratic and was transferred to the Hawthorne Hospital for the Insane in 1862 under the care of progressive Dr. James Hawthorne. He advocated for more fresh air and less punishment than commonly used in such institutions up to that point. Indeed, one of her

Prisoners using the laundry facilities. On the left is shown a basket of folded laundry, and on the right women are washing clothing in a large tub. *From the* Queenslander, *November 28, 1903.*

descendants maintains that the transfer was a humane measure rather than a punitive one. While at Hawthorne, Charity was observed to have achieved a measure of peace:

> *Among the notables we saw in the Female Ward was Mrs. Charity Lamb, who killed her husband several years ago. She sat knitting as the party went through the hall, with a face imperturbably fixed in half-smiling contentment, and apparently as satisfied with her lot as the happiest of sane people are with theirs.*

She died on September 16, 1879. At the time, her cause of death was marked as "apoplexy," what is now defined as "unconsciousness or incapacity resulting from a cerebral hemorrhage or stroke." Charity was buried in an unmarked grave at the Hawthorne asylum. In 2008, records were examined by a mental health advocacy group, and it was discovered that she might have been one of more than one hundred asylum residents to be buried underneath a parking lot adjacent to Portland's Lone Fir Cemetery.

She was buried in what is now called "Block 14," for those too poor to afford their own burials, and adjacent to the grave sites earmarked for the Chinese section. Excavators presume that the graves, which were packed tightly in rows and paid for by the state with a five-dollar fee, may have had wooden markers that disintegrated over the years. Around the 1930s, the graves were covered over with pavement, and a building was put up on the site in 1955 but torn down in 2004. As of time of this writing, Portland Metro had just finished fundraising to create a memorial for those buried in the Block 14 area.

Each of them, including Charity Lamb, will be identified by name.

EDMUND CREFFIELD

WILD AND CRAZY TIMES WITH THE BRIDES OF CHRIST

E dmund Creffield is compelling even in the slightly mad pose of his "mug shot," or intake shot, at the Oregon State Penitentiary, where his pose is much more casual than his situation would infer. His look does not necessarily convey the animal magnetism that his followers were recorded as seeing or the allure his teenage "wives" saw. His intense gaze and spare, muscular frame look more frightening or chaotic than that of a ladies' man. The wide smile on his lips doesn't match the unhinged look in his wide eyes. Whichever way you saw him, in person it must have been difficult to look away.

Franz Edmund Creffield, sometimes known as "Joseph," immigrated to the United States after he became a deserter from the German army around 1900 or 1901. He landed in Portland, and the main public knowledge is from his involvement in the local Salvation Army there. Creffield was stationed in other towns for the Salvation Army and resigned from working with the organization in September 1901 to pursue a more committed religious lifestyle.

He spent time traveling as a preacher for a year afterward but made a permanent home in Corvallis, Oregon, at the end of 1902. Something about his preaching style drew people to him. Creffield spoke about simple living and adherence to the Bible—especially according to his interpretation of it. Simplicity became austerity. During his sermons, he would get worked up into a frenzy. The people who followed him, mostly women, gave up their possessions, sometimes burning them, and lived together communally.

Right: Sign for Lone Fir
Cemetery in southeast
Portland, Oregon, 2012.
Mike Krzeszak.

Below: Portland, Oregon
waterfront, 1898. *Herbert A.
Hale, Library of Congress.*

Rumors of orgies held nightly were sometimes vaguely corroborated, but much was made of the free love aspect of the groups in the press. They were unkempt, dressed in very little. One of the most important ideals was the belief that Edmund was actually "Joseph" or "Joshua," a man who succeeded Moses and had "the power to 'intercede' between heaven and those on earth." He preached about free love and peace, and surely his multiple weekly services provided respite to the women and girls who flocked there, particularly relief from the chores, activities and people who controlled them in other aspects of their lives.

His mission was to bring nonbelievers into his fold and awaken them to the way of life that would be their salvation, according to him. That included not just adherence to his biblical teachings and non-reliance on possessions but also shutting out those who were not followers. This created hardships within families, but some families joined with multiple members. Those who participated were dissuaded from sitting on chairs or benches, instead sitting on the floor.

Those who followed him became known as "Holy Rollers." Within Creffield's group, it referred to two things. The first was the practice of people rolling around at his feet during services in religious fervor. The second was Creffield's statement that those who followed him would have their names written on the "Holy Rolls" of heaven. He called the group the "Brides of Christ."

One of the things that alarmed the community of Corvallis was how many prominent members appeared to fall under Creffield's spell. Orlando Victor Hurt, who was the manager at Kline's Department Store, the largest department store in the area, joined along with his wife, Sarah; twenty-two-year-old daughter, Maud; twenty-one-year-old son, Frank; and sixteen-year-old daughter, May. Hurt figured large not only in the community but also in the Republican committees of both the state and county. Other prominent people in the group included Donna Starr, twenty-five, and Esther Mitchell, fifteen, sisters of George Mitchell. They were said to have become very close with Creffield, but the group denied any impropriety under the guise of their free love doctrine. A man named "Charles Brooks" was his second in command and was also an ex-member of the Salvation Army in Corvallis. Others drifted in and out of the Holy Rollers, not staying long enough to be mentioned in print as of importance.

He preached for hours on end, sometimes throughout the night. The racket got louder as his ranks swelled. Eventually, the group was banned from Corvallis proper, and they moved to the previous summer residence of the Chepenefa Kalapuya tribe, known as Kiger Island today. Creffield's teachings became more controlling. The congregation was manipulated into submission by the lack of food and sleep. Anyone who disobeyed the tenets was cast out.

As the weather grew worse in the fall, the group was invited to live with the Hurt family. Signs posted at the door and other locations outside the home read, "Positively no admittance except on God's business." Rumors flew through the community that the group had graduated to burning children, but they were false. They burned many other items in the family home, like heirlooms, utensils, linens, furniture and even a cat and dog:

Certain caprices of religious fanaticism have been manifested at the house that are so unusual as to suggest a condition bordering insanity. Walks about the house have been torn away. Much of the furniture in the house has been reduced to ashes, on a theory that God wills it. The shrubbery and fruit trees about the yard, and all the flowers have been digged up and destroyed. Kitchen utensils have been beaten to pieces and buried.

Those weren't the only items destroyed. In Creffield's quest to control the sect, most items that would be considered of luxury or comfort were cast aside, including "guitars, mandolins, chairs, window curtains…and carpets." The animal "sacrifice" was later found to be a "humane disposal" of a dog. Mr. Hurt reported that it was killed because it was unwanted and wouldn't go away and that it was later thrown in a refuse fire. Corvallis residents were uneasy with all the rumors and would at times stand outside the home straining to get a glimpse of what was going on inside. As a result, wire and gates were strung up to keep people away.

In late October 1903, enough complaints had been made about the group that the two male leaders, Creffield and Brooks, were arrested:

A popular belief is that Creffield is a Hypnotist, and that it is to his hypnotic influence that most of the conditions are due. When Brooks and Creffield were taken into custody, the officers found most of the residents lying about on the floor on mats, blankets, and other places of rest. In the center was a young girl with a cloth over her face, apparently in a trance. She was at the moment receiving a message from on high, which others about the room were taking down. The head of Creffield was close beside that of the youthful message-taker.

That evening, under cover of darkness, a mob assembled outside the Hurt residence and stoned the building. What started as a torrent of small stones grew larger, and the glass in the windows was broken out. Two men knocked forcefully at the door and, when there was no answer, knocked the glass out of the door too. After the crowd got no more response and all the lights inside were turned out, they left and weren't prosecuted for the acts.

The women in the group were asked to give up any fine clothing. In exchange, they wore simple brown dresses. No one brushed their hair. No one wore stockings or shoes, and in fact, they went barefoot everywhere. Creffield began to seduce the women in the group to look for the "second mother of Christ." In some cases, the "free love" extended to both a mother and daughter. The *Evening Telegram* reported that it was unbelievable that he would "live in the same locked house with a number of your girls and do nothing in the world but be religious." These women's families were splintered.

Creffield and Charles Brooks were captured and tarred and feathered by a group of local men who were called the White Caps in January 1904. Brooks disappeared after that but was later found in the woods outside Albany with two other church members:

> *Lounging carelessly around their campfire were the three religious fanatics, intensely interested in perusing the pages of three well-worn Bibles and discussing questions of theology. A few dirty blankets and dry boughs served for beds, while a couple of tin cans comprised the stock of culinary utensils. Their food was limited to a scanty supply of potatoes, a small sack of wheat and a little coffee. Here these three eccentric worshipers had subsisted for a week and they appeared happy and contented with their meager and uninviting surroundings.*

Brooks and company were ordered to leave and were last seen going toward the border of Marion County. Creffield ran off after the tarring and was tenderly cared for by church members, including his new wife, Maud (Hurt) Creffield, whom he married the day after the tarring "in a room where the odor of tar was noticeable." He went to Seattle and after a time made his secretive way back to Corvallis.

By February 1904, Creffield and Maud's aunt, Donna Starr, were accused of having an affair in Portland. Since adultery was a criminal act, a warrant was issued to arrest him. He successfully ran away and concealed his whereabouts for many months, even though men were actively looking for him throughout the state.

While he was in hiding, his flock fasted and prayed, lying on the floor, prostrate in their faith. Some of them were sent to the Portland Boys and Girls Aid Society. Frank and Mollie Hurt, Maud Hurt-Creffield, Sophia Hartley, Attie Bray, May Hurt and Rose Seeley were first to be committed. Others, including Cora Hartley, were sent to the Oregon State Insane Asylum. Sarah Hurt was sent to the asylum in June 1904. In July, Creffield was "found nude and starving under her house," where he had been hiding:

> *Creffield's time under the building was spent in a hole in the ground under the northeast corner of the house. It is three months or more ago that Creffield fled from Portland officers and disappeared from*

view. The hole in the ground is alongside the brick foundation, and is six feet long, eighteen inches deep and two and a half feet wide. The northeast corner was apparently selected because it is the darkest place under the house.

In the hole there was a pillow and two old bed quilts. Under the pillow were a pair of old drawers and a shirt. These were the only articles the apostle had to keep him warm. The dirt from the hole had been leveled off, and under it were found eleven half gallon and seven quart fruit jars, all empty, save that in one there was a little sugar, in another a little flour, and in several decayed remains of a little uneaten fruit. A small tin cup had butter in it, and another showed that it had been used for stirring flour. In one of the jars fruit and flour had been stirred together. These articles with a knife and spoon, all hidden under the dirt completed the naked apostle's commissary department.

Despite his claims of innocence, he was found guilty and served seventeen months in the Oregon State Penitentiary. During that time, Maud divorced him, but they remained friendly, and she visited him in the penitentiary.

When he was released in December 1905 due to his self-reported "good behavior," he declared that he was the reincarnation of Jesus Christ and that his prison release mimicked Christ's resurrection. He and Maud remarried, and from there they traveled to San Jose, California, to various places in California and then to Seattle. From right after the time when he was imprisoned to the time he was released, he sent letters to newer followers, the Seely girls in Oregon City, for redistribution to his former followers. Through these letters, he apparently regained his position as a strangely appealing ladies' man right away.

Another curious revelation was born from Creffield's imprisonment. He claimed that he was responsible for calling down the 1906 San Francisco Earthquake. What's more, he said that there was more to come. His followers flocked back to him and sent many letters to him in return. There was seemingly no break in their affections. Cora Hartley, an ardent new follower, said in an interview:

Creffield is Jesus Christ. He condemned the city of San Francisco and brought the earthquake; he has condemned the city of Corvallis and an earthquake will destroy this place.

San Francisco, April 18, 1906, from "As I Remember." *Arnold Genthe, Online Archive of California.*

His absence from the town he formerly called home did not go unnoticed by the newspapers either:

> When questioned why Joshua Creffield hired a team at Airlie and drove through to Wrenn Station, instead of passing through Corvallis on the train en route to the coast, the witnesses stated that "Creffield, who is the Holy Ghost, has condemned Corvallis, and that he never returns to a city that he has condemned."
>
> Perhaps the memory of a warm coat of tar and feathers supplied by Corvallis citizens one fine night something over two years ago may have decided Joshua to travel by private conveyance.

His followers set up a new camp at his direction on the Oregon coast below Ten-Mile Creek near Waldport, and according to the papers, they were "simply awaiting the commands of God, and that they will be governed accordingly." Creffield traveled with Maud safely by private train and boat to avoid notice. The Ten-Mile Creek area was said by Creffield to be safe from the dangers that had caused him to condemn other areas.

The Hartley mother and her daughter attempted to rejoin them as soon as he set up the call for his former followers. They were thwarted by Cora Hartley's husband, Louis Hartley, who had been following them. Mr. Hartley found them at the train station as they departed the Newport area to meet up with the group on the coast. They saw him at the station, ran away

Elevation view of the Ten-Mile Creek Bridge, view looking east, 2004. *Library of Congress.*

from him and concealed themselves in a room at a local farmhouse overnight to hide until the next morning. They disappeared before dawn to catch the early ferry and left a shiny half dollar on the table as payment. Their aim, of course, was to reach Creffield and his camp and evade Louis Hartley.

When Hartley realized that they had slipped away, he hoped to catch them before they reached the ferry. He went to a sports goods store and procured a gun. Upon reaching the ferry landing, he saw Creffield on board, standing at the boat rail, accompanied by his wife and daughter.

Hartley twice fired his gun at Creffield, but it didn't work. He would later write in his divorce decree that "owing to the fact of rim cartridges instead of center fire cartridges that happy event [shooting Creffield] was avoided by the flight of the said Prophet." He was not the only one who was looking for the followers of Creffield.

The *Morning Oregonian* reported that upon setting up the coastal camp, "they were immediately followed by many of the women of Benton County, who had been under the spell of the 'prophet,' and the orgies of the Holy Rollers were reported to have begun again." The newspapers weren't shy of predicting doom either. Many called for Creffield to beware in case some more angry husbands would care to come after him, and certainly legal recourse of some kind was vaguely alluded to. It was clear that the general populace was not at all willing to accept the strange practices of the group and believed that something bad would come of it. It all reads today as a concern bordering on nosiness, but was it actual concern about mental illness or only tabloid interest? Creffield and his followers were kept apart from infecting the rest of the community by putting them in the jail and insane asylum, respectively. There seemed to be a larger question now that they were reunited about how to socially control them and keep the movement from spreading to more women and families.

All that changed a few days later. On May 17, 1906, Creffield and his wife, Maud, were walking down the street in Seattle, Maud being in the market for some new clothing. As they walked up to the Quick Drug Store, George Mitchell, Maud and Esther's brother, came up to the

Oregon Dunes, 1980. *Carol Highsmith, Photographs in the Carol M. Highsmith Archive, Library of Congress, Prints and Photographs Division.*

couple and shot Creffield through the back of the head with a .22-caliber revolver at 7:10 a.m. The bullet exited through his right eye, killing the man instantly.

Even as he hit the ground, Maud "refused to believe that he was dead," according to bystanders. She was so firm in her belief that Creffield was a holy man that she could not grasp that he was gone. On her knees she cried, "Speak to me, Joshua," and looked intently at him until those present moved him inside.

She stood in the drugstore, where they moved the body to keep it safe from curious onlookers, mute and probably in shock. Maud was described as "rather stout, short in stature and plainly dressed," with large blue eyes. She would not consent to have her photograph taken until she could clean up, comb her hair and get ready for it.

Patrolman Le Count had been near the scene of the crime when it happened and had witnessed the shot as well as Creffield's collapse. As he ran to the scene from a block or so away, he saw Mitchell, calm, smoking a cigar. Upon his arrest, Mitchell handed over the weapon without fuss and said, "I came to Seattle on the Wednesday morning train from Portland. I came here for the purpose of killing Creffield. I saw them on First Ave. this morning and shot the man. That is all there is to it. He ruined my two sisters, and I took his life."

George Mitchell. Photo is from a newspaper article subtitled, "He Ruined My Two Sisters, and I Took His Life." *From the* Seattle Star, *May 7, 1906.*

Mitchell kept his cool and was forthright with the police officers once he was brought to the station. He answered everything they asked him and was calm. He had been searching for Creffield for some time. A group of people from the families of those who followed Creffield was loosely connected in trying to find and "deprogram" their loved ones from his teachings. One of them was Maud Hurt Creffield's father. One of the first few things Mitchell did at the jail was to send him a telegram: "I got my man. Am now in jail. —George."

Officers brought Maud to collect their things from where they had been living. It was a cheap boardinghouse, sparsely furnished, and she collected her even more meager possessions. All she owned in the world was on her person and wrapped in a newspaper: some combs, paper and writing utensils, a Bible, a pistol, cartridges for the gun that had been in Maud's pocket and a package of tobacco. She defended their lack by saying they were going to look for work. She gave the law fake names and insisted that there was no reason Mitchell would have for killing Edmund Creffield. She was put in the charge of the female prison matron and housed there.

Reactions from the public to Creffield's death pulled no punches in their approval of his being stopped, as noted in a May 8, 1906 article, "Slayer's Sister Carried Messenges," in the *Morning Oregonian*:

> *It is not an over-statement of the fact to say that the news of the death in Seattle this morning of Creffield was received her with universal satisfaction. With him removed, there will be no "Holy Rollerism" here or anywhere.*

The *Corvallis Gazette* on May 11, 1906, printed a plea to raise money for Mitchell's defense. A group of men from Corvallis, headed by Maud Hurt

Creffield's father, O.V. Hurt, even raised enough to buy and present Mitchell with a medal when he went to Seattle to support his daughter and possibly bring her home.

Maud Hurt Creffield still refused to think her husband dead for certain, even when she buried him in a state-supplied pine coffin. She thought he would rise again in four days and was confident in that assertion to multiple newspapers. His other followers were similarly convinced when they saw him at the morgue. Maud also asserted that if she had had her gun in her pocket, not just the cartridges, George Mitchell would be the one lying dead. She waited at his grave for the four days and was perplexed when he did not come back to life. Maud continued to be angry with her father, brothers and anyone who was trying to vilify Creffield.

Five women and one small baby were found waiting for Creffield a few days after his death, starving, on Heceta Beach on the coast. They didn't believe reports of his demise and were waiting for him to come back, eating only crabs and mussels that they harvested from the sea. They were rescued by a local farmer who wanted nothing to do with them for fear their "Holy Rollerism" would spread.

The trial of George Mitchell began in late June 1906. After a drama-filled trial—including juror illness, a judge being murdered, fanatic defense of the cult leader and plenty of testimony against Creffield—George Mitchell was found not guilty on July 10.

Only two days later, as Mitchell was about to get on a train to where he was to be re-employed at his old job, his sister Esther, seventeen, showed up unexpectedly. Esther had waited to see George and their brother Fred at the station's entrance before the train left. At 4:25 p.m., she greeted them. Fred asked her, "Won't you say good-bye to George before he goes away?"

Esther shook his hand, nodded and said, "Goodbye." Fred offered to take the coat over her arm, which happened to be concealing a gun. She gave him the coat. In that instant, she turned to shoot her brother George in much the same place as he had shot Creffield. He died at once.

After she was arrested, she revealed that the crime had been committed in league with Maud Hurt Creffield. Maud and Esther waited for their trial in jail, at various times being reported as sick with typhoid fever, which was false, or stomach-related ailments. Once they were allowed to see each other, they were happier and were apparently treated as well as possible in the circumstances. They were said to be comforted by sleeping together, each embracing the other, and Esther often sat by the side of Maud's bed.

During the trials, which happened in September of that year, Maud appeared unwell. The two petitioned to be tried separately, and it was granted. At Maud's trial, she testified that:

> *Until two days before the killing I intended to do it, knowing it was God's will that I should do so. At that time Esther came to me and said that God had made known to her that it was his will that she should kill her brother, George. Both of us had been in a state of prayer. I did not believe her. I was certain that it was God's will that I should do the killing. However, both of us again entered into a state of prayer and it was witnesseth to me that Esther was correct and that it was God's will that she should do the killing.*

Both used a defense of insanity. Press and popular sentiment were by turns scathing and sympathetic. In addition to the coverage of George Mitchell's crime itself, this phenomenon was something Rosemary Gartner and Jim Phillips wrote about in their paper in the *Pacific Northwest Quarterly*. It was called "the unwritten law," the idea that an outraged husband, father or brother could justifiably kill the alleged libertine who had been sexually intimate with the defendant's wife, daughter or sister.

While awaiting the trials' long ins and outs, Maud Hurt Creffield waited in their cell. The evening of November 16, 1906, Maud visited the restroom and used a cold footbath, and the two went to bed on the same cot as per usual shortly after 10:00 p.m. Around eleven o'clock, guards heard Esther scream. They entered the cell to find Maud lying in the bed, dead. The first opinion as to cause of death was heart disease. By November 21, the results of the autopsy and chemical analysis showed something very different. Maud had died from strychnine poisoning. Esther was vehement that Maud would not kill herself and that everything in the cell and on her person was searched, but the poison is lethal in as small a dose as an eighth of a gram, and nothing was found.

Esther was convicted of insanity and sent to the state asylum in February 1907. She was considered "cured" and released into her father O.V. Hurt's care in April 1909. Although she married in March 1913, she was restless, and she committed suicide by taking strychnine herself in August 1914.

The Holy Rollers gradually disbanded since their leader was murdered, and Esther left her worldly goods to her husband and sister.

MRS. EMMA HANNAH

FURY, INDEED

The world of the 1890s held the promise of the Gilded Age and the hope of a new world, and the Progressive era was upon us, even if those promises didn't always reach as far as rural Oregon. The Transcontinental Railroad was operating a second line; the game of basketball had been invented in 1891; and General Electric, the Sierra Club and Yosemite National Park had all been created. Things were changing, but not quickly, in outlying areas. Female beauty standards were strict.

In modern times, we wouldn't take a woman wearing pants for anything but just that. In 1895, the idea was so preposterous that Mrs. Emma Hannah was able to use that to her advantage to hide in plain sight, by simply wearing male attire, and commit murder. The difference between the two types of attire is vast.

The woman in question, Mrs. Emma Hannah, had a long-standing feud with Charlotte "Lottie" Hiatt, who was heard to have said about her one day that "she had rather have cut Mrs. Hiatt's throat than have her in the hop yard." There was clearly a long animosity between the two.

Later, in 1897, Emma Hannah would be examined to determine her sanity:

Declared Insane.
Mrs. Hannah, a Lifetime Convict, Committed to the Asylum
Late Friday afternoon, Mrs. Emma G. Hannah was examined as to her sanity, and as a result of the examination the woman was committed to the insane asylum…

The woman was received at the penitentiary from Linn County in
November 1895, under life sentence, having been convicted of the murder
of Mrs. Lottie G. Hiatt, near Scio, on September 26, of that same year.
Mrs. Hannah was today transferred from the penitentiary to the asylum.
If she shall recover the law requires that she be restored to the prison to
serve out her sentence, which is life.

How did she get from dislike, albeit vehement, to murder and then to an insane asylum? One of the main places to put women who killed (or women who were otherwise criminal, or for a variety of other reasons) was in the asylum. Otherwise, it was off to the Oregon State Penitentiary, as a female-only facility; Oregon Women's Correctional Center wasn't built until 1965 and the Coffee Creek Correctional Facility in 2002. But why did Emma hate Charlotte so much? The answer was love, or possibly insecurity about the younger woman perhaps. While we won't ever know exactly, the newspapers had a field day with the sordid tale when Emma killed the rival for her husband's affections. Many wanted to find a reason beyond what might have seemed obvious.

As the *Wheeling Register* put it, "Particulars of the tragedy by which Mrs. Lottie Hiatt was shot and fatally injured at her home near Scio, a small and remote town in Lynn County, furnish a very strange story of a woman's murderous jealousy."

Emma Hannah married her husband, John, in 1879, at age twenty-nine, a somewhat late age for marriage in that era. She and John had four children. Emma was reportedly in pain or possibly chronically ill, and it may have been that that pushed her into such a rage against her husband's perceived infidelity. Their marriage was not reported as either bad or good before Lottie Hiatt caught her husband's eye.

Several children and six years later, having decided that her husband was being unfaithful, or at least that he was paying an awful lot of attention to attractive Mrs. Lottie Hiatt, Emma walked over to the Holman home disguised in men's clothing—an oversized coat, a hat and glasses. She presented herself rather emphatically as a "book-agent," but the family declined to purchase a book or newspaper. The figure, who had appeared near dark, forced their way inside and, when they closed the door, demanded to know where to find all the money that belonged to the family. The *San Francisco Call* alleged that "the purpose of the assault was robbery, as Mrs. Hannah knew the elder Mrs. Hiatt, who lived in the home, had collected $500 on a note that afternoon." They would not give over any money, however.

Trees and clouds—a typical Oregon view, 1942. *Russell Lee, Library of Congress, Prints and Photographs Division.*

Lottie Hiatt's mother-in-law, Mrs. Hiatt, who was eighty-two at the time, got angry at the rude request. She grabbed a piece of firewood and hit the intruder right in the face. "He" knocked her down in return, and she fell with a bloody scalp wound.

The intruder, Mrs. Hannah, quickly took out the revolver she had hidden beneath her coat and shot at the women, who forced her outside and into the yard. The shots were later found lodged in the doorframe. She knocked the elder Mrs. Holman, Lottie Hiatt's mother and roommate, unconscious with the butt of her gun. Lottie herself was on the verge of fleeing into the night, but Mrs. Hannah shot her twice in the back of the head. The two gunshots killed her quickly as she lay on the ground of her yard. Hannah was discovered because she had left the hat she had been wearing where it had been knocked off her head by the elder Mrs. Holman at the scene of the crime, and the glasses and outfit she had been wearing were recognized as belonging to a relative of Mrs. Hannah's. The bruises she sported because of the struggle were damning as well. "Mrs. Hannah bears the marks on her face the marks of the blow from the stick in the hands of Mrs. Hiatt's mother," the *Lebanon Express* reported, and "she admitted enough to show that she did the shooting, but she and her husband now deny that she was away from home that evening at all."

A peculiar thing in this case is that there was a precedent in the area for the man who committed adultery with another woman to be punished. Theoretically, Emma Hannah could have waited, and the punishment would have taken its course.

Another adultery case was only as far away as Eugene, perhaps sixty miles, but it might as well have been worlds away if nobody involved read the newspapers. On July 12, 1884, a woman called Louisa Babb engaged in adultery with a man named Sid Horn. By her own admission, "the defendant, whom she did not like, nor look upon as her friend, and, not desiring to be seen by others, she remained in the woods with the defendant until about 9 o'clock that evening, during which time she had sexual intercourse with him; that while in his company they ate a lunch consisting of pickles, cheese, cold beef, and bread."

The Babb/Horn couple went on to meet several more times. Curiously, in the appeal, the meals they ate were mentioned often: "pickles, cheese, cold beer, and bread" or "sandwiches, pickles, cheese and cake." Sid Horn was convicted of adultery and sentenced to the penitentiary for one year, but it was reversed on appeal. There was certainly news both printed throughout the state and most likely by word of mouth demonstrating that the male part of an adulterous relationship could be punished.

But was someone like Emma Hannah likely to have access to any of that, let alone reading the newspapers? Male and female attire were very different at that time, even in places that kept up with the latest fashion, and the audacity of Emma to don male clothing to disguise herself was novel given the cultural constraints if not the purpose.

There is no written evidence of Mrs. Emma Hannah's state of mind during the court proceedings in the trial against her. The newspaper's view of how she behaved during the trial is chilling to say the least:

In the Hannah case, J.R. Wyatt [Emma Hannah's lawyer] *stated that application for a new trial had been filed on the usual statutory grounds. Without argument the court denied the same and an appeal will be taken at once to the supreme court. The defendant was asked to stand, when Judge Burnett made the only sentence in his power, imprisonment in the state penitentiary for life. The defendant received it as undisturbed as if it had been an invitation to dinner. Mrs. Hannah will now take up residence in the suburbs of Salem, one woman among several hundred men, the beginning of an isolated, lonely life, unless given a new trial.*

Elsewhere in the same newspaper, the author mentioned how "[h]er family bid her good-bye, and all promised to visit her in the penitentiary. The opinion is general that after a few years' imprisonment she will be pardoned. They don't like to keep women in the penitentiary any longer than they can help. Penitentiaries are not built for them."

It is hard not to extrapolate, but it seems by reading between the lines that at least this paper commiserated with Emma Hannah. The *Lebanon Express*, among others, called out her victim in its article, saying, "Mrs. Lottie Hiatt—a divorced woman—was shot at her mother's home."

Vintage beauty advertisement, date unknown. *Collection of Karen Watson.*

It is thought-provoking to consider that her divorcée status was worthy of mention in the very first line of that article. But consider at that time that only about 1 percent of all women in the United States, over all age groups of married (white) women, were divorced in 1895. Not only was divorce a cultural rarity and a moral question, but it was also not a practical choice. Economists of many political and moral types agree that the importance of the family as a labor unit was disrupted as women became more independent in economic means through employment. This explains in part why the murder was so extremely shocking—it was undermining the whole agreed-upon fabric of the way things worked. It was disrupting two families' livelihood as well as relationships.

Love affairs outside marriage surely happened then as now, but no evidence ever came to light of an affair between Lottie and John as fact. The rumor mill had it that anonymous notes were left on Emma's fence post alleging the relationship between John and Lottie, and that's how Emma found out. Such a note was never determined to have existed, and a motive or sender of such notes was never disclosed. Lottie's son, Lofa, reported seeing the killer having gray hair, a bun, a hat and glasses, the latter two of which were found to belong to Emma's son, and she had borrowed her husband's coat.

Her trial started on November 25, taking place soon after the murder on September 26. Emma Hannah's husband, John, disappears in the newspapers after the events, and he is not much mentioned in the trial. In the trial, Mrs. Hannah was swiftly condemned. While her act was not right, her feeling of jealousy and of feeling slighted seemed to have been seen as understandable given the coverage.

After her conviction, Emma Hannah was remanded to the Oregon State Prison. She was transferred to the Oregon State Insane Asylum in 1897 and went back to the penitentiary before coming to the asylum for the remainder of her life. She died there in 1930.

DAYTON LEROY ROGERS

DANGER IN THE FOREST

The Molalla Forest Killer started off early, according to Michael Newton in *An Encyclopedia of Modern Serial Killers*: "At 16 he was arrested for shooting at passing cars with a BB gun."

Dayton Leroy Rogers was only eighteen when he attacked his first victim, his girlfriend, in 1972. The girl, unnamed in newspaper reports because she was a minor, was only fifteen years old when she was stabbed after the pair went to a remote area near Eugene, Oregon, to have sex. He pleaded guilty to the attack, during which he had the girl "close her eyes, and then plunging the knife into her belly." She was one of the lucky ones. Persuaded to take her to the hospital, he reluctantly did so and was charged with second-degree assault. He received four months' probation.

That teen was only the first known victim in the long career of the man who has been dubbed "Oregon's Worst Serial Killer." The attack was the first known in Rogers's Willamette Valley string of bizarre attacks and murders, perhaps motivated by a strange fetish.

A year later, he was caught after assaulting two Lane County–area girls, also fifteen at the time, with a soda bottle. After this attack, his next stop was the state mental hospital. He was let out of the hospital in 1974 and embarked on a more than ten-year-long killing spree.

The years 1983 to 1987 held especially dark secrets. Rogers would prowl the streets of Oregon, searching for women who were easy targets. Author Gary C. King wrote in his book *Blood Lust: Portrait of a Serial Sex Killer* that while prowling on the streets, Rogers called himself by the name "Steve" and introduced himself as a professional gambler. He was enamored of prostitutes because heroin addicts were needy and easier to fool. Rogers picked women up off the street, but the expected transaction of sex for money would not occur. Instead, he drove them to various parts of the forest, where he poured miniature airline-size bottles of vodka into glasses of orange juice. One of his preferred beverages was small—portable Smirnoff vodka and orange juice that came in bottles with green pull-top caps.

Then Rogers would hogtie, gag and assault the women. Rogers's next court appearances came in May 1976, when he was acquitted of rape, and in August of the same year, when he was also acquitted of rape. He had tied up two girls in the back of his car and assaulted them.

Rogers started out as a Woodburn, Oregon–based businessman, a businessman with secrets and a peculiar fixation with women's feet. His attack, torture and murder of Jennifer Lisa Smith outside a Denny's in Oak Grove got him convicted and sent to prison for life. The Molalla Forest atrocities got him sentenced to death.

Dayton Leroy Rogers frequented Portland's prostitutes. According to author Gary C. King in his book about Rogers, *Blood Lust: Portrait of a Serial Sex Killer*, he was afflicted with something called "bloodlust." The condition only went away when he wounded or cut another person or caused them pain. He got a headache with "blinding white pain," and "the only way to make them go away was to let his dark side fully emerge."

His rages belied the otherwise quiet engine repair business owner, husband and father to a small boy. He had started going out in the evenings while his docile, religious, quiet wife and their son slept. His excuses were pileups of work that he and his assistant couldn't get done in their regular working hours. His jaunts turned into visiting the working girls who lined the streets, particularly Union Avenue, which was then an area where it was known that all kinds of appetites could be satisfied.

Jennifer Smith had the bad luck to be the woman who got in Rogers's Nissan pickup truck on August 7, 1987, in Oak Grove. He paid her the agreed-on forty dollars for sex, including bondage, took her to an empty lot and bound her feet and hands with shoelaces. Then he left the car to relieve himself. As he did, Jennifer untied her bindings and found a knife in the glove box. When he reentered the car, he said she attacked and tried to take his wallet. They wrestled for the knife, and when he got it, "I got a hold of it and used the knife on her. I was just going back and forth in any direction I could."

She managed to get out of the car, run to a nearby Denny's parking lot and call for help. He tackled her, and people from the restaurant and nearby bars came to her aid, seeing Rogers still attempting to assault her. He ran away. One of the witnesses who had tried to help Jennifer did see the attacker's license plate number after he tried to stop his car from getting away. She lived for a brief time but died from her wounds. Clackamas County detective John Turner led the charge to find and apprehend Rogers.

He was later convicted of Jennifer's murder, given life in prison and was in custody that August when the Molalla Forest remains were discovered. Detective Michael Machado was one of the first policeman to see them. A bow hunter, Everett Lee Banyard, hunting deer southeast of the town of Molalla, Oregon, found a hand sticking out of the soil in the deep forest, and Detective Machado was first on the scene.

The assumption was that the remains were of one individual. Then Machado saw another body nearby. The first victim was Reatha Marie Gyles, sixteen, and the second, found in a fetal position, was Lisa Marie Mock, twenty-three. Gyles was reported to be a prostitute from the Portland area. Both bodies were leathery and mummified, said Machado.

Shortly thereafter, they gridded the forest area to search. A few minutes later, they found two more bodies. Further searching revealed that several were mummified or almost so, and three of the women were missing one or both feet, which had been cut off at the ankle. The third body was cut from sternum to pelvis. Many days of searching gave up varied clues to the killer. Ropes, hair, collars that looked like dog collars, shoelaces, plastic bottles and miniature Smirnoff vodka bottles were strewn around several body sites. As their search widened, Machado said that they smelled "a strong, pungent, overpowering odor." One of the most important pieces of evidence was a Regency Sheffield kitchen knife, which had been reported by witnesses at the Denny's as the one Rogers had been holding as he escaped by climbing over a chain link fence en route to his car.

The sixth body, when they found it, was in pieces. Two of the previous bodies had deep wounds and cuts in the abdomen area. This one was just hair and ribs—no torso, legs or feet were on site. Nearby was the old and decomposed body of victim no. 7.

The painstaking process that the detective and police teams used to collect evidence and interviews culminated in a trial for the deaths of all six women on March 30, 1989. According to Senior Forensic Science Research Manager Robert Johnson at the National Institute of Justice, serology, fabric and tool analysis, tool mark comparisons and hair analysis were used to make the

View of the Molalla River from walking trail, at Molalla River State Park, Oregon, 2009. *Luteguy, Wikimedia Commons.*

case. The trial did not shy away from the torture Rogers inflicted on his victims. They had been bitten, apparently to cause them to bleed, cut and eviscerated; in some cases, the injuries were thought to occur premortem. At least thirteen to fifteen women testified that they had all been treated similarly to the dead women and were able to describe their experiences in detail. His penchant for bondage and rough treatment was chilling. One woman testified:

> *"He was biting and tearing. I told him to please stop. That's too rough. This isn't right! I cried and begged for him to stop. And the more I pleaded and begged, the worse the abuse got. When I screamed too loudly, he became concerned and put something up against my neck, which I assumed was a knife. He told me to be quiet, or else I'd really have something to cry about. I didn't say anything, and I tried to stifle the sobs as much as I could." "Did you say anything to the defendant?" asked Eglitis. "No." "What were you doing then?" "Just existing."*

He was found guilty of aggravated murder on all counts. It had taken the jury only hours to decide that the evidence to that effect was overwhelming. In the sentencing phase on June 7, 1989, it took a little longer, but the jury concluded that he would be sentenced to death by lethal injection. The names of the women buried in the Molalla Forest were twenty-three-year-old Lisa Marie Mock, twenty-six-year-old Maureen Ann Hodges, thirty-five-year-old Christine Lotus Adams, twenty-year-old Cynthia De Vore, twenty-six-year-old Nondace "Noni" Cervantes and sixteen-year-old Reatha Gyles. The seventh victim he has been tied to in the forest was identified in 2013 as eighteen-year-old Tawnia Jarie Johnston.

The Oregon Supreme Court overruled his case twice because of technicalities at the time of trial. These penalties were reinstated by juries, although lethal injection has since been outlawed, and the sentences were commuted to life in prison. His latest appeal to have his sentences overturned was scheduled for March 5, 2021. His death sentence is still overturned, but he must serve all six life sentences consecutively.

Dayton Leroy Rogers is incarcerated at the Oregon State Penitentiary. During his time in prison, similar abusive behavior patterns caused authorities to warn at his parole hearings that he would no doubt continue his murder spree if released, on possibly both men and women. He is reportedly a barber for the inmates there. He was sentenced to death four times: in 1989, 1994, 2006 and 2015. The *Oregonian* reported:

> *During his 2015 resentencing hearing, Rogers admitted killing a seventh woman, Tawnia Jarie Johnston. Her body was found in the Molalla Forest with the other victims, but she wasn't identified until 2013. In a statement to the jury, Rogers said Johnston was one of the "precious lives I have taken."*

He is suspected of killing at least one more victim who has yet to be found.

FAMILY OF THE CHILDREN OF THE VALLEY OF LIFE

CULTS, CAVES AND CARNAGE

Best. Eugene. Cult. Ever.

In 1975, a family of sorts was freed from the series of caves they had been living in Lorane, a tiny logging town near Eugene, Oregon. The caves had been dug by hand—literally by digging out dirt with their hands, it was said—and the Family of the Children of the Valley of Life were hiding from the authorities. This time in hiding would not be the last time the group was allowed to take refuge with its cofounder, Norman "Snake" Brooks.

Along with Snake, the other cofounder of the group, Jeanne Gilmore, had started the group in 1968 in Los Angeles "as a way to give young people a chance to stay out of trouble," according to an article about them in the *Idaho State Journal*. What transpired, mayhem that included a cross-county chase and hand-digging a rabbit warren of caves to live in, didn't exactly fit that agenda.

In 1942, Reverend Norman Thurlow "Snake" Brooks was born in Austin, Texas. He was raised by only women, his grandmother and mother, and never knew his father. Life in Austin at the time was brutal for a Black man. A particularly horrific account of his life from that time was recalled in an article for *One Dollar Magazine* from February 1976: "He was told in detail about a nearby slaughter of black people by a group of Texans; he was horrified and carried the memory into his adulthood."

As a young man, he was ordained as a minister in his family's Baptist church. For a short time, he was its pastor, but he left both the state and the church career behind as he traveled west in the United States. He worked in restaurants, in hotels, as a chauffeur and eventually as a musician. He had stints in jail for car theft and said that "he was trying to get caught to learn the jail experience."

During his time as a musician in California, in which he said he was successful enough to be both a studio musician and record his own (unreleased) album, he met Jeanne Gilmore in the later 1960s. They lived together and took in runaways to make their "family," one that authorities would say resembled the Manson Family. Brooks and Gilmore's reach was mainly reserved for those family members who followed the call to join them in the large home where they lived, where they were cared for by Jeanne, nicknamed "Mommie," and revered Brooks as a father figure. The group flourished in the "free love" era of the late 1960s, and the girls came from all over the Los Angeles area and elsewhere to see them. Gilmore was the owner of a chain of women's stores and helped finance the group, and others brought their life savings with them to share. The group grew as more girls entered, leaving jobs, schools and families to join them, seduced by the ethos of acceptance and love that Snake preached. He would later say that the group was formed to keep kids out of trouble. Rumbles grew about their relationships and the way they chose to live communally.

Brooks and company visited places all through the country, trying to find somewhere to make a permanent home where they could live as they pleased. They looked around in various places to find people like them. In 1969, they thought they'd found it in Port Angeles, Washington. There they met Belinda Lederer. Originally from Missouri, Lederer had finished college and spent her early years wanting to be a nun. The Brooks family and their commitment to good works appealed to Lederer, and she became committed

The Haight-Ashbury neighborhood, San Francisco, California, 2016. *Arjun Sarup.*

to them and Brooks quickly. After a time in Port Angeles, their home and shop burned to the ground. Group members claimed that it was arson by unhappy townspeople in retribution for their lifestyle.

Undeterred, they hitchhiked down to Eugene, Oregon. Several more women joined up there. One of the newer acolytes was particularly valuable, a woman who joined with a $320,000 inheritance from her timber-wealthy family, along with another from a wealthy country club family. Both were considered assets to contribute to the family's upkeep. Lederer and Snake had a son during this time, whom they named Unicef, while another woman and Snake had a son named Univass.

Lederer and Brooks started a chain of restaurants called Lighter Brown, Darker Brown. They featured plain food and good portions but absurdly low prices. To set the standard of the time, the McDonald's menu from 1972 would sell you a Big Mac for $0.65, an order of fries for $0.26 and coffee for $0.15. LSDS, as it was called, sold meals at a much lower price, like a cup of coffee for a nickel and other foods accordingly. Followers were encouraged to work there.

The philosophy of the Children of the Valley of Life was printed on the menus:

> It's true today that the most important thing in business is to show as much profit as possible, usually money, but the "Lighter Brown, Darker Brown" owners are interested in a different kind of profit. Things that don't show up on the cash register. This is a family of people that only wants to give people a chance to find their own happiness. They came to Eugene to start a restaurant with prices everyone could afford and 24-hour service so no matter the time of day or night a person gets hungry or just lonely, he or she will have someplace to go.

The food was plain but good, and the restaurant was indeed open twenty-four hours a day, with free delivery. Deliveries were quite slow, though, and it was well known to sometimes not be quite all that you had paid for. A Eugene resident said as much:

> Lighter Brown, Darker Brown was real alright. I used to order their food delivered in the middle of the night (free delivery 24 hours a day with no minimum). LBDB drivers were known to eat parts of your order, i.e. French fries. Deliveries were not fast. People said bad things about Snake but we never saw the evidence. I was very sorry to see LBDB go.

If it seemed unsustainable and sketchy, it was understandable that the restaurant garnered unwelcome publicity. Snake claimed that a large amount of money had been stolen from a safe in one of the restaurants, and with one thing and another, the ventures closed. Couple that with the group's stated goal of helping kids turn away from juvenile delinquency and people started to notice.

The next venture for the family was a children's television show. They continued trying to help kids and garner public support with other charitable activities, like free breakfasts at the park. It proved less successful than they had hoped. The public suspected prostitution, a long-standing belief about the group that had followed them as they had grown, and a mysterious, but never verified, underground connection that was possibly the thing that helped them make so much money. Much of the money came from the generosity of its members, including some inheritances that the group put to good use. The group's varied makeup was remarked on in newspapers as well, as it included "two former Catholic nuns, a teacher, and a doctor."

Snake Brooks was reported as saying that "wiretapping, informers, and hidden microphones were being used to entrap him." The group's privacy and Brooks' need for control led them to next live in even more rural Oregon, in a log cabin. Eventually, the home was raided, and the children were removed temporarily due to unsanitary conditions in 1973 in an investigation headed by Detective Roy Dirks.

The result was weeks in temporary housing for the children until they could go back to their family. Brooks and company felt persecuted by Dirks, perhaps because of that incident and perhaps because of Snake's increasing paranoia. A protracted battle with authorities brought the children home again. The year 1974 brought them back to the Lorane, Oregon area, where they made their homes in an elaborate system of hand-dug caves, which they continued to work on and dig out. Pat Edwards mentioned in her book *Sawdust & Cider to Wine: A History of Lorane, Oregon & the Siuslaw Valley*:

> They moved into two separate large caves on Bureau of Land Management land. The first of the two was believed to have been originally built by Clarence Roemhild and Lee Alldridge in their search for gold. The second cave was elaborately decorated when it was discovered. An article in the Eugene Register-Guard described the caves. "The caves had a series of tunnels that went about 50 feet into the hillside. The main room was oval,

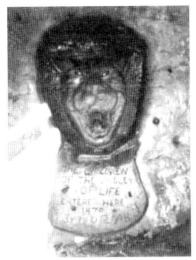

Left: Children of the Valley of Life carving, 1975. Carvings were found in the hand-dug cave system in Lorane, Oregon. *Private collection of Mel Keep.*

Right: Snake carving in the Children of the Valley of Life caves, Lorane, Oregon, 1975. *Private collection of Mel Keep.*

> about 15 x 20 feet, with a 12-foot ceiling supported by log beams. The walls bore large carvings of animal and human figures and one carving bore the inscription 'The Children of the Valley of Life; Entered Here 1974; By Norman.'"

Townspeople say that the caves may have been originally built by local native tribes before Roemhild and Alldridge used them, but this was not corroborated. Belinda said that she was one of the sculptors in some newspaper articles, and other articles do not name the artists other than to say they were quite talented. Other stories from Lorane residents have the family members walking down the country roads barely clothed or wearing seasonally inappropriate summer dresses as they walked to the store during a snowstorm. The country residents tried to be welcoming to the family, but their strange behavior was off-putting, and they were confused about why they lived underground.

Newspapers described the hand-dug home further, saying, "Bureau of Land Management employees, who were notified that the group was living in the caves on BLM land without permission, said heads of cats and figures of women were carved into the earthen walls. There was also a seven-foot statue of a man resembling Brooks."

The relationship between Brooks and Gilmore was a husband/wife arrangement, as was the case with seventeen other women in the group who called themselves Brooks's wives. The communal living family had six children between them as well, although only two of them were Brooks's. The family pretty much kept to themselves, according to Lorane residents. The women were leery of outsiders, both due to the seizure of the children and because Snake was having them all practice shooting with guns, something not all of them were comfortable with.

Snake was arrested for carrying an unlicensed firearm in late February 1975. Shortly afterward, they decided to head out to the woods for good, to be a family, together and away from those who judged them. They drifted away to live in the forests around the Eugene/Springfield area, with the idea to live off the land as best they could.

On April 16, 1975, they had started to set up camp in a clearing off an isolated logging road, a landing near the mouth of the Blue River Reservoir and dam. Family members were gathering near their transportation, a hand-painted van, then broken down. Some of them were stationed at the mouth of the road to warn the others in case anyone should show up to harass them.

It was a surprise, to say the least, to see Detective Roy Dirks pull in, although the group was increasingly wary. Detective Dirks was reportedly

Blue River Reservation in the Cascade Mountains, 2011. *Gary Halvorson, Oregon State Archives.*

a good man and a dedicated officer. At thirty-eight, he was a decorated policeman who was searching for clues or witnesses in a drowning nearby related to a cocaine case he was working on.

Detective Bill Kennedy was Dirks's partner at the time. He was grateful to have worked with Dirks on the Brooks case, as he was a good detective and an empathic one. "Brooks was something like Charles Manson," he described him, "a manipulative sociopath."

When Dirks got out of the car to confront Snake and company that day in 1975, he was greeted with the armed sentries and then Snake himself. The situation was tense. Dirks denied being there specifically to hassle the group, but rather he was there investigating a drowning nearby and saw the broken-down van that led him to the encampment.

One of the women cried foul, and Dirks replied that his incident notes from the drowning investigation in his car would prove what he said. She then dove into the front seat to look at his notes. The other guard, Belinda Lederer, was nearby. As one of the mothers of Snake's children, she was invested in his well-being on a different level. The woman in the police car verified Dirks's claim with his notes but turned off the police radio. She may have also grabbed the keys—accounts vary.

Dirks, perhaps thinking that she was going for the ignition, turned back to the car and went to get the keys or turn the radio back on. Snake turned to bar his access to that direction, possibly in confusion, possibly to protect the woman in the car, and lifted his shotgun. Dirks deflected the rifle Snake held and quickly drew his own weapon.

Belinda Lederer sighted her own weapon. She aimed and fired at Detective Roy Dirks, hitting him in the head and killing him instantly. A witness said that his head was half blown off. Whether her motive was fear, a feeling of self-preservation or otherwise, she had killed the man whom the family saw as the greatest threat.

In the immediate aftermath, the group hid Dirks's body. Several of the people present were sick seeing the carnage; Belinda Lederer is noteworthy at having been reported as violently sick. They piled branches and sticks over him and ran away on foot. Brooks and Belinda Lederer were found and arrested hitchhiking along the side of the road outside Blue River, Oregon, west of Eugene, as Sheriff David Burks said to the *Oregon Daily Emerald* newspaper.

The bulk of the group ran as far and fast as they could through the wilderness but were found "frostbitten and hungry" after three days around sixty miles away from Eugene. All the women were arrested due to the condition of the children, weary and cold after the three-day hike in the cold and snow. They were considered "hindering prosecution" after the crime.

Although he had not held the gun that killed Dirks or was even within twenty-five feet of the weapon, Brooks was sentenced to five years for hindering prosecution. Both newspaper and magazine articles alleged that racism and misunderstanding had something to do with his sentence. The family women, save Lederer, were released, arrested again for refusal to testify against Brooks and released again. They lived together in Salem for some time.

Belinda Lederer was found guilty of manslaughter and sentenced to ten years, the maximum allowable sentence for that crime. She was later interviewed by a psychologist, who said that she shot Dirks during extreme distress and was operating under the assumption that they were in fear of their lives. Later, after she changed her last name to avoid notoriety, she lived in Lahaina, Hawaii, and became a gallery owner.

A circuit court transcription from March 11, 2003, is an interesting bookend to this story. Roy Dirks's estate brought a wrongful death suit against Brooks in 1975 and the property and money she and Norman "Snake" Brooks possessed. Beverly Brooks (then known as Beverly Felice Benton Daugherty) had first met Brooks in 1973 when her daughter, Maureen Daugherty, was living with the group. For the next two years, she visited her daughter and the group at least monthly. Beverly moved out from her husband's home and in with the family in July 1975. In January 1976, she obtained a divorce from her husband, Dr. Robert Daugherty, and in December of that year was given a settlement of $300,000 in cash. Beverly legally changed her name to Beverly Happy Brooks in August 1975, while Maureen changed hers to Merry Brooks.

Beverly and Snake decided to move the family away from the area in January/February 1976 and that he would go there when he was released from jail. Beverly went to Maui with a briefcase full of $150,000 cash to procure a property for them in both their names. When she found an unimproved property for $100,000, she wanted it to go to her godchildren, Snake Brooks's children, in the event of their death. As he had no will, the real estate agent told her that the easiest way would be to put his name on the deed. She did not engage a lawyer to help with the purchase and never mentioned buying the property in a trust for the children. The escrow agents were informed by Beverly that she and Norman "Snake" Brooks were husband and wife, since she saw him as her life partner and thought that they met the definition of being married.

She and Norman were listed on all the documents as co-owners, married partners and joint tenants. She went back to Oregon to visit Snake in jail to tell him about the property. At that time, she met with an Oregon attorney who said that she could get his name removed from the deed, but she deemed it unimportant and never did so. During 1976, Norman Brooks and Beverly Brooks signed papers witnessed by a notary in Oregon that authorized utility easements on the Hawaii property, and Norman designed a home that was built on the land. Norman Brooks was let out of jail on August 10, 1978, and moved to the property on Maui.

Just a short time later, on August 29, 1979, the wrongful death lawsuit was settled in Roy Dirks's estate's favor, and they were "awarded damages totaling $1,200,000" according to the court transcript. Because they weren't legally married, their attempt to retroactively change the deed was denied, and they were ordered to pay the damages, with costs.

Norman and Beverly Brooks started a "fish farm/water holding/jungle park," and he became a fine art photographer. Brooks died in Maui on December 17, 2016.

The Lane County Sheriff's Hall of Honor memorialized Dirks on its website with the following:

Detective Roy Dirks
April 11, 1975
In Memory Of…"Those who asked so little and sacrificed so much."

Detective Roy H. Dirks was investigating a drowning incident in the Blue River area when he was shot and killed by Belinda Lederer, a member of the Norman "Snake" Brooks family. Lederer was convicted of manslaughter and Brooks was convicted of hindering prosecution. Suspects belonged to a communal group that had prior contacts with Detective Dirks. Roy previously was a resident deputy in the Cottage Grove area.

ROY "VIC" SUTHERLAND AND DULEY THE WRESTLING COP

ALCOHOL AND ANARCHY

I n 1930s Eugene and Springfield, posters advertised a local wrestling match all over town. At the post office, or on a shop window, they hailed hometown hero "Duley, the Wrestling Cop" and his battle with his next opponent.

On Tuesday, November 25, 1930, his promising boxing career, as well as his long-standing career upholding the law as a policeman, were cut short by moonshiner Ray "Vic" Sutherland. Duley was an accomplished policeman. Records of him arresting bootleggers, being a member of the Royal Neighbors fraternal organization, assisting the Railroad Traffic Police and being a celebrated local wrestler speak to his community engagement.

Ray, known more often as "Vic," was born on August 27, 1867, to George Henry Sutherland and Mary Jane Henry in Grant County, Wisconsin. He was the second of three children born to the couple. He married Flora May Reed on June 20, 1897, in Liberty Vernon County, Wisconsin. He got involved in the underground moonshine business, presumably between then and the time he settled in Oregon.

The life of a moonshiner began way earlier than the common misconception of Prohibition-era United States. It's an industry that has existed as long as there has been starch and yeast to ferment and distill. In the earliest times of our country, folks commonly brewed to provide themselves and their neighbors with alcohol. Home brewers were taxed after the Revolutionary War to help the government pay its bills; it was repealed in 1802 and then renewed to help pay for the next war, the War of

Brown Jug gas station, 1980. *Part of the John Margolies Roadside America Photograph Archive (1972–2008), Library of Congress.*

1812. It was repealed again but put in place once more in 1861 to help pay for the costs of the Civil War. In the American South, the liquor-brewing culture was seen as part of its history and legacy, according to author K.M. McCann, who said, "The alcohol taxes applied post–Civil War were viewed by Southerners as an extension of Yankee tyranny. As such, local Southern politicians did little to enforce the laws on moonshiners.… During the '50s and '60s, one out of every five gallons of liquor in America was moonshine."

The culture of the United States post–Civil War was a permissive, look-the-other-way attitude. Prohibition-era liquor distributors started to change their cars to both carry loads of liquor and evade the federal agents and police. Booze was a lucrative business, after all, all over the United States, Prohibition or not. However, it was the only way many families made money, and they were reluctant to stop. And it was the business of the police and federal agents to hunt them down for the public good.

Ray Sutherland's family was thoroughly involved in the business. His sons helped deliver, if not produce, the moonshine. His sons certainly were questioned in the salacious murder that led to the end of the elder Sutherland and indicted in transporting it.

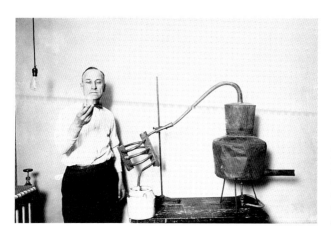

Internal Revenue Bureau inspects the contents of a recently confiscated moonshine still, 1930s. *Farm Security Administration.*

It all started with the moonshine. Distributors crisscrossed the United States and up and down back roads to evade the policemen and government agents in specially kitted-out cars that had large, often concealed, cargo areas for the purpose. On the night of August 29, 1930, Officers Oscar Duley and John Carlisle were informed of a party at the Sutherland residence. They crept up to watch nearby and waited to follow the expected moonshine delivery that night from the Sutherland clan. Ray Sutherland and his son Baude drove the delivery vehicle down Marcus-Wendling Road outside Marcola, Oregon.

A group of young men approached the vehicle looking to buy. Baude Sutherland was sitting in the front seat of the car holding a jug of moonshine in his hand when he was arrested by Officer Duley. The unidentified youths saw Duley then shot down by Ray Sutherland through the window as he was stepping on the running boards of the vehicle, and the killer himself was wounded the hand when the other officers returned fire. The group of potential buyers left as quickly as they could, tearing down the dirt road to Marcola to let authorities know. The *Roseburg News-Review* reported, "Duley, with five bullet holes in his body, was tossed to the side of the road. Sutherland and his son disappeared. [Officer] Carlisle, hearing the shots, found Duley alive and conscious and rushed him to Eugene to a hospital where he died after midnight."

Several hours later, during the day, Sheriff Harry L. Bown led a posse to raid the Sutherland home in Marcola. Along with his son, Deputy Lee Bown, they attempted to draw out the moonshiners. The posse used bloodhounds to track the men, and the trail led back to the Sutherland residence. The two-story frame house/store across from the Marcola Post Office was surrounded by the officers and volunteers who made up the posse. The

Above: Seneca, Oregon. Loading cattle hides onto a truck, 1942. *Russell Lee, Library of Congress, Prints and Photographs Division.*

Left: Side of Cates's new house, sporting a large skull. This was a typical, if quirky, look of homes in the 1930s and 1940s for rural Oregon, 1939. *Dorothea Lange, Farm Security Administration— Office of War Information Photograph Collection, Library of Congress.*

Sears sign in rural Oregon, 1941. *Russell Lee, Library of Congress, Prints and Photographs Division.*

policemen opened to door of the home to retrieve Sutherland, but they were forced away when Ray Sutherland opened fire.

Game Warden Joe Saunders was killed instantly. Deputy Lee Bown and Deputy Rodney Roach both were shot and hospitalized with serious wounds. Lee Bown was shot in both legs, while Roach received shots in a foot as well as both arms. Sutherland was believed to have been hiding under the floor of the home, according to the blood trail that the tracking dogs identified. His son Baude was arrested a few hours later in Marcola. Baude said his father ran off out the back into the thick forest between Marcola and Wendling after the deputies were killed and before they descended into the home.

Douglas County sheriff V.T. Jackson and prison superintendent Harry W. Meyers offered to help find the fugitive, and a county-wide manhunt began. On September 11, 1930, Baude Sutherland was indicted for bootlegging. The public had expected a more serious count, as in murder or conspiracy to commit murder, but it was found that the stronger case was in the illegal liquor charge. His father, Ray Sutherland, was indicted in absentia for four counts, the two murders of Saunders and Duley and "assault with intent to kill" in the cases of Bown and Roach. The deputies were later discharged and recuperating.

By September, the public had become more concerned, and efforts were increasing to catch Ray. On September 15, 1930, Governor Albin Norblad issued a reward of $250 for information that would assist the capture of the killer. "The Hunt has resolved," the *Capitol Journal* said, "largely how long Sutherland can endure into a question of waiting to see how long a life in the wilds without food and with a wounded hand." Reports of him were made as far as Portland and down to Eugene, but none panned out. He was thought to be hiding on a farm near the home of his ex-wife and that she had helped him, but she denied all claims of doing so.

The public became inflamed with sightings, although most turned out to be false. On November 20, 1930, the frenzy got another man arrested. A freezing man was found outside in the area where Ray Sutherland had been seen before and was thought to be hiding, but it turned out that he was just a man living rough in the dirt-floored wooden cabin. Rumors flew that another death in the valley was attributable to Sutherland, that of a man who happened to see him on the run, but it was never proven.

Not long after that arrest, on November 25, Sutherland was finally caught. He had come to the forest near West Fir and spent his daylight hours in a cabin. At night, he retreated to a cozy, nicely constructed lean-to sheltered with branches all around to conceal it. That evening, a posse caught wind of where he might be and approached the lean-to. They had been asked to take him alive if possible and called out to him. Sutherland, surprised, started to

Walnut growing in Oregon, 1910. *Jacob Calvin Cooper, Farm Security Administration.*

Oakridge, Oregon railroad tracks, near where the shootout to capture Ray Sutherland took place, 1942. *Russell Lee, Library of Congress, Prints and Photographs Division.*

fire on them as soon as he saw them approach. Deputy John Carlyle and his son, Deputy Lester Carlyle, returned the gunshots and "poured a withering fire" into his lair.

Sutherland, shooting with his left arm and holding his wounded right arm to his chest, shot blindly, and they went wild. The Carlyles shot him dead. The intense search was finally over. Deputies were astonished at how well-appointed his cabin and lean-to were.

After learning about his father's death while he himself was in custody at the Kelly Butte Rock Pile, Baude Sutherland expressed no surprise. He said that Ray Sutherland "was a pretty good fellow to me" and that "I was never with him long, but he always treated me all right."

Left: Square Deal Farm, Willamette Valley. Part of a photo serries chronicling the American people, 1939. *Dorothea Lange, Farm Security Administration.*

Below: Railroad warning sign in rural Oregon, 1941. *Russell Lee, Library of Congress, Prints and Photographs Division.*

One interesting thing to note was that Baude exonerated Ray Sutherland in some things. Baude may have been simply shielding his father or felt that he had nothing to lose, as he was already imprisoned. The truth of it may never come out. He said, "That was all bunk about him running a still. He didn't know how to make whiskey. I know because he asked me several times to do it.…So far as I know dad hadn't been handling liquor until a short time ago and then he sold only a few bottles. He had always been quite a gambler but I don't think he sold whiskey before."

Ray Sutherland's death was not mourned by the public. In fact, the general attitude reported by newspapers was that justice had been well and truly done. In an "Oregon Briefs" news short titled "Old Wounds Found," the *Oregon Statesman* wrote with relish:

> *Eugene, OR., November 26—(AP)—An Inquest into the death of Ray Sutherland, 47, who was killed in a posse near West Fir yesterday, will be held here tomorrow, Coroner Bastedder announced today.*
>
> *Physicians who performed an autopsy today said that the top part of Sutherland's head had been shot away, both hands had been hit, and several bullets had entered his body. Old wounds, believed to have been from previous bullet wounds, were found.*

The papers, typical of the day, continued to dispense heavy-handed proselytizing as they moralized after he was gone. "There is only one lesson taught by the misspent life of Ray Sutherland and its tragic end," intoned the *Evening Herald* on November 28, 1930. "It is a lesson young men will do well to ponder over. Continue a life of crime and you will pay with your life. It is inescapable."

JEROME BRUDOS

SHOES AND SLAUGHTER

Jerome Brudos was born on January 31, 1939, in Webster, South Dakota. His reign of terror may have had its genesis there, but it was mainly in Oregon where the serial killer prowled for easy prey. He was the serial killer who lived the longest in the Oregon state penal system until his death on May 28, 2006. Although his crimes weren't fresh in the minds of Oregonians at the time of this writing in 2022, the case is one as obscene today as it was more than fifty years ago.

The two boys in the family, Larry and Jerry Brudos, had strict parents whose behavior certainly helped give the second of the children severe issues later in life. Their mother, Aileen, had wanted a girl for her second child, and so she was recklessly cruel to both children, especially to Jerome. They would later report emotional and physical abuse at her hands. Their father, Henry, was only intermittently present in their lives. That left them both at the mercy of Aileen much of the time. The family moved around quite a bit in his childhood and spent time in South Dakota, Oregon and California and then eventually made a more permanent home back in Salem, Oregon.

What is thought to be the primary instance of Jerry's later fetishizing of women's shoes occurred when he was only five years old. He was apparently browsing through a junkyard near their home in Portland and found a pair of women's high-heeled shoes. Fascinated, he wore the shoes home. His mother, Aileen, berated him and was so angry that she "took the shoes off his feet and burnt [them]," according to author Nehita Abraham.

Aileen Brudos beat him severely for the transgression, hoping that this would solve the problem.

When the family moved next, to Riverton, California, Jerry got in trouble because he stole his first-grade teacher's shoes from the classroom. Then his family moved twice more by the time he was twelve years old, first to Grants Pass, Oregon. He developed a habit there of sneaking into the neighbor's home to raid the clothing and underwear of the neighbor's daughters. He would collect more undergarments and shoes from various sources to keep for his own use. The family later moved to Wallace Pond, Oregon. Once, a teen girl, who thought she was with Jerry as a friend, fell asleep on his bed and woke

Ribbon tie shoe graphic from advertisement, 1880. *Collection of Karen Watson.*

up to him trying to take off their shoes. In his early teenage years, Brudos stalked young girls his age, knocked them out, stole their shoes and ran off with the footwear.

As he became a teenager, Jerry Brudos grew more and more dangerous. In 1956, he was seventeen years old. He dug a deep hole in a hillside and planned to hold girls inside there as sexual slaves. "As he matured, his shoe fetish increasingly provided sexual arousal," said author Eric W. Hickey in his book *Serial Murderers and Their Victims.*

A seventeen-year-old girl was the first unlucky target of the hillside hideaway. He kidnapped the girl at knifepoint while he was wearing a mask. He tried to make her take off her clothes so he could take photos of her. She refused and he became enraged, beating up the girl. After he allowed her to put her clothes back on, he left and then "accidentally" ran into the girl, telling her that the real perpetrator had locked him up elsewhere and he'd just gotten out.

He was seen by an older couple coming out of the hillside. He was caught and as a result was put in the Oregon State Psychiatric Ward for observation. His first diagnosis, later deemed inaccurate, was of "adjustment reaction of adolescence with sexual deviants and fetishes." Doctors were less alarmed by the women's clothing and lingerie he had accumulated and more worried about the way he dreamed about placing girls he kidnapped in freezers arranged in salacious positions.

His stay there was not long. After less than a year, he was released with the diagnosis of borderline schizophrenia. He moved home and finished high school. Incredibly, the army accepted him in 1959, when he was twenty. He was thrown out of the army for what Frazier said in his book was "sexual obsessions."

Brudos had been trained as an electronic technician and found work in that field. He met a girl, seventeen, who has been referred to as "Ralphine," "Darcie" and "Susan" by various sources, but the consensus is that her name was Darcie Metzler. They married and had two children of their own. The family went mainly unnoticed and were seen as a "regular" family. Jerry was seen as a man who didn't generally curse, drink or smoke.

Darcie was made to act out some of Jerry's wishes. He asked her to do housework in the nude, wearing only high heels, and photograph her as she did so. She eventually grew weary of his demands and stopped acquiescing. She spent her time caring for their two children instead of giving in to him. The couple stopped sleeping in the same bedroom.

In 1967, he started walking the streets of Corvallis at night, stealing underwear and shoes when possible and peeping in windows, sometimes at the dorms of Oregon State University. He said that he was having severe migraine headaches and "blackouts" and that his nighttime tours relived that pain. Some reports say that he started wearing women's clothes more frequently. A woman and her shoes caught his eye one night. He followed her, raped her and strangled her, leaving with her shoes. Luckily, his victim was not dead, that time. He wasn't caught and combed the papers for mentions of the crime. At night, he would keep up his "walks" through the university neighborhood, watching.

The next victim conveniently came to Brudos instead of him having to scour the streets looking for her. On the afternoon on January 26, 1968, when his family was upstairs, an encyclopedia salesman named Linda Slawson came to the house. Once he had her inside on the pretense of purchasing the encyclopedias, he knocked her out with a piece of wood. Then he strangled her until she died.

Brudos hid Slawson's body in his workshop/garage, which the family was told never to enter. Jerry had used extreme threats in the past to make sure this was the case. He posed and photographed her body using female underwear that he had stolen and then cut off her foot as a macabre souvenir and hid it in a freezer in the garage. He would later use the frozen foot to model his collection of high-heeled shoes. Not long after he killed her, he took her body, tied it to a car engine and took it to the Willamette River to dump.

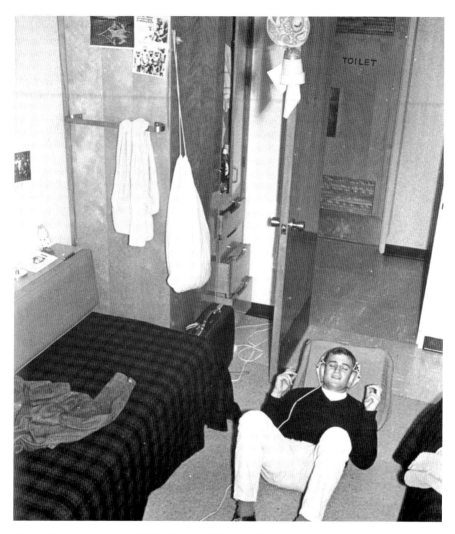

Oregon State dorm room, 1968. *From the OSU yearbook.*

On November 26, 1968, he helped his next victim, Jan Susan Whitney. The twenty-three-year-old woman had a car problem on Interstate 5 between Albany and Salem, and he told Whitney that she could call a tow truck at his house. Once he got her in his vehicle, he strangled and raped her. He removed her breasts to use as paperweight molds after he finished with her body, and then he tied a railroad iron to her body to dispose of her in the Willamette River. Along with Whitney's remains, he threw away Slawson's foot, which had decomposed significantly by that point.

Barbershop, Monroe, Oregon, 1980. *John Margolies Roadside America Photograph Archive (1972–2008), Library of Congress, Prints and Photographs Division.*

On March 27, 1969, he kidnapped eighteen-year-old Karen Sprinker from the parking garage of a department store. He took her to his garage, forced her to be photographed in his stolen underwear and then raped and strangled her. He used nylon cord to tie Sprinker to a car engine and threw it into the Willamette.

Brudos tried to abduct two women at knifepoint from department store parking lots. Sharon Wood, twenty-four, and Gloria Gene Smith, fifteen, both escaped him in April 1969, Wood on April 21 and Smith on April 22.

On April 23, 1969, he managed to kidnap Linda Salee from the parking lot of a department store. He took her home. He killed her there, abused her corpse and posed her in his underwear collection but decided not to remove her breasts. After she died, he tried to animate her with electrical currents but was unsuccessful. Her disposal was conducted in the Willamette again, this time by lashing her to a car transmission. Her body was found a few weeks later down the Long Tom River by a fisherman, tied to the transmission with distinctive knots. Police continued to scour the river for clues and found the mutilated body of Karen Sprinker.

The investigation revealed that a suspicious man had been corresponding with students at nearby Oregon State University. He called himself a

The bucolic Long Tom River, where Brudos dumped several of his victims, 2021. *Pithecanthropus4152, Wikimedia Commons.*

Vietnam vet and was searching for dates. His conversations with the women were unsettling. At one point, he "mentioned the bodies in the river and had made an unsettling suggestion about how he could strangle her."

Police cooperated with the women to set a trap for Brudos, who had given the women false information. They were able to obtain a search warrant for his home on their suspicions. In his garage, they found copper wire that matched some found on the bodies. It was shown to have been cut with the same tools. Along with the rope, some matching the rope on the bodies, they found his heinous souvenirs and photos of the crimes. Brudos was arrested partially on the strength of the specific knot used, and he confessed to four of the murders. During his confession, he also talked about his earlier assaults and attempted crimes.

Brudos was tried and convicted of Sprinker, Whitney and Salee's murders on June 28, 1969. The way he tied the knots and the rope he used were both key elements in determining that he had committed the atrocities, as were similarities to the types of automotive and other equipment he had tied to the women in order to conceal the evidence. He was not charged with the murder of Slawson, whose body was never found. His punishment was three consecutive life sentences.

Darcie, who divorced Brudos after he was arrested, was charged with aiding and abetting him in the crimes. She denied any knowledge of his crimes or participation in them. After all, she wasn't allowed to even enter the garage. Brudos had installed an intercom she was required to call him with if she wanted to go in or communicate with him there. The charges were dropped against her in October 1969. She said, "He has to be sick. I don't think any person in his right mind could do the things he did and not be sick. I don't have the ability to know the extent of his sickness, but I know he is ill." She changed her name and moved herself and their children somewhere where they could live anonymously.

While he was incarcerated, Brudos collected piles of shoe catalogues that he kept in his cell. When he attempted to get parole in 1995, the request was denied, and he was told that parole in his case would never be granted.

Brudos contracted liver cancer while incarcerated. On March 28, 2006, he died in jail. At the time of his death, he was the longest-incarcerated individual in the Oregon Department of Corrections.

The horrific case of Jerry Brudos, the Long Tom River Killer, has been told elsewhere in print (notably by Ann Rule in her 1983 book *Lust Killer*) but was also more recently the inspiration for the series *Mindhunter* and the performance of actor Ted Levine as Buffalo Bill in the film *The Silence of the Lambs*. He remains one of Oregon's most horrifying serial killers.

POLICE CHIEF JOSEPH STILES

DECEPTION AND DISASTER

Chief of Police Suicides," the headline read on March 16, 1906, in the small Eugene newspaper. "Joseph Stiles, of Eugene, Charged with Statutory Crime, Takes the Short Cut."

It was the end of an unlikely story for the forty-seven-year-old chief of police, one that unfortunately affected his wife and children. The chief had been well regarded and worked during many years for the department. He came from Winterset, Madison County, Iowa, where he was born on January 19, 1855. He married Sadie in 1880, and they moved to Eugene in 1894. Appointed as chief of police in 1887, he later resigned to run for sheriff as a Republican. After he was defeated, he went back to his former job as chief of police, where he served until his untimely death. A member of various fraternal organizations, Stiles was well thought of and recognized as an efficient and trustworthy "criminal catcher," a churchgoer and a man with many friends.

The shortcut in mention in the headline was the fact that Stiles shot himself in the head with a revolver on the evening of March 8 and was found in a downtown business's shed the next morning. At the time, he was being investigated under the statutory charges by two young girls, Erma, fifteen, and Ruby Miller, sixteen.

He had last been seen the night before the trial was to begin in the vicinity of the cannery downtown at about nine o'clock, pacing and walking the streets, and he was not seen again. Two weeks before, he and Virgil Rowland, a constable of the Eugene Justice District, alongside two other men, were

At the Police Station, 1906. Ink pen by Per Fredrik Röding, Stockholms Stadsmuseum, Sweden.

"Telephones and telegraphs (and municipal electric fire alarm and police patrol systems), 1906." While Eugene's police department was not as luxurious as this, an up-to-date police station such as Eugene's would have looked similar at this time. *U.S. Bureau of the Census, William Mott Steuart (1861), Thomas Commerford Martin (1856–1924), Arthur Vaughan Abbott (1854) and William Mayer.*

seen and supposed to be having affairs with the two girls. It was intimated in several places, though never shown to be factual, that assignations were held in the offices of the police station or its back rooms and that wild card parties were held there on his say-so:

> The friends of the two men refused to believe the stories and thought the affair was nothing more than a blackmailing scheme. The rumor became more and more intense, and two of the young men involved left town, fearing arrest. It is said that those two, threatened with persecution, started the story regarding Stiles and Rowland.

The evening he took his own life, everything good in his previous existence must have seemed to unravel as the indictment for the "debauchment of the girls" loomed. Witnesses saw him, upset as he walked around, although "he seemed jovial, and spoke with many friends, his station of mind was plainly not." It is insinuated in the newspapers that he had been drinking downtown and was distraught at the thought of facing the trial. Stiles took himself to the local tannery and shot himself point-blank in the head "at the east end of Elizabeth Street."

The coroner went on to say that as Stiles's body lay on the ground in full dress uniform, "stretched out full length with his head resting on the boards," the chief's brand-new .32-caliber Colt was still within reach of his right hand. The paper didn't stint on the gruesome details either. "Two holes in the head showed where the bullets had plowed through the brain. It entered about an inch and a little back of the right [ear] and came out almost directly [in front]." Other sources stated that the holes could be seen "through the temples from right to left."

The rumors of Rowland and Stiles's behavior was rather an open secret within the Eugene community, or so it would seem. The *Morning Oregonian* went on to report:

> The story that the two peace officers [Stiles and Morgan], *as well as several well-known young men about town, had been in the habit of indulging in nocturnal orgies with the Miller girls had been gossiped about for weeks and was laid before the grand jury when it met by P.I. Miller, the father of the wayward damsels. On the first charge, Rowland was arrested and held under $500.00 bonds. On the adultery charge he was held under $1500.00 bail.*

Eugene, Oregon residences, 1906. The fine homes in town would have looked like this. *Brück & Sohn in Meißen.*

The thought of the indictment must have been truly terrifying. Stiles, as he walked about the area, was visibly upset after the indictment of Rowland was read. He was not seen again after 11:00 p.m. until he was found by Mr. W.W. Haines, who passed the area as he was taking his horse to pasture.

After Stiles was transported to Gordon's morgue, very near the courthouse as it happened, they inventoried the contents of his belongings. The police station, which took up a large section of the downtown block it occupied, was still inhabited with his colleagues, who had to investigate both Stiles and the case involving him and Rowland.

The coroner found two notes written on paper in his pockets. The first, written in a general sense to the Eugene citizens, said:

I cannot stand this disgrace, and I am not guilty. So Good-bye to all.

The note to his wife was even sadder:

Sadie:

Take good care of the boys. Forget me as soon as possible. With love to all, I bid you Good-bye.

JOE.

As sad as that part of the story is, the plot thickens. The two other men seen in the company of Stiles and Rowland were arrested in Jacksonville, Oregon, 165 miles away. Brothers Lauren and Lawrence Farlow "got wind of the probable action of the jury" in Rowland's case and ran away from Eugene several days before the term of court adjourned. A small two-paragraph article was tucked in the corner in the same issue as Stiles's suicide was featured. It announced, "These are the young men indicted the other day for giving liquor to the Miller girls and are the ones that are said to have induced the girls to swear that Chief of Police Stiles and Constable Rowland were mixed up in the scandal that has led the Chief to take his own life."

The Farlow brothers were brought to civil court on the morning of March 16, 1906. The trial proceedings, which were reported, were exhaustive, and a blow-by-blow account of the events was given. After being "charged with giving liquor to the Miller girls" at 8:00 a.m., when court convened, they gave the boys until 9:00 a.m. to plead their case. Meanwhile, the jurors for the court that day were gathered, and the *State v. Virgil Rowland* case began. He was charged with adultery with Ruby Miller. Eighteen-year-old Ruby Miller took the stand, and when the "cool and collected" witness was questioned, said that she indeed stayed with Rowland on one night in October 1905. She testified that she had also stayed with him in December 1904, April 1905 and July 1905 and that intimate relations did occur. Ms. Miller said that he was not the only man she had stayed with and emphatically noted that at no time did she sleep with Chief J.S. Stiles. Her sister, Erma, who was sixteen at the time, testified next that she slept in the room with her sister and Rowland and participated in drinking beer with them and with others.

The girls' father, P.L. Miller, was next to testify, followed by his wife. Using the family Bible, they affirmed the girls' ages. Mr. Miller also said he was trying to find evidence as to who had given the girls alcohol when he found they had been drinking. Virgil Rowland's father, J.T. Rowland, testified as well to his son's age and status of his marriage.

The man who took over for Stiles as sheriff, E.A. Farrington, was next to testify. He said that he had known Rowland for more than twenty years and that he had told him that he had a relationship with Ruby Miller.

The most shocking person to speak in Stiles's favor was revealed by the *Eugene Weekly Guard*:

> ### Note and Comment
> *There is one man who does not believe Joe Stiles guilty of the charge made by the girls, and that is the man is a most competent witness in defense of the honor of the dead—Dr. T.W. Harris. He had been treating Stiles for two years for impotency, and asserts that the physical evidences were such that to his mind any sentiment of wrongdoing in that way was the basest calumny…just about two months ago, Stiles came to him greatly discouraged and said he had lost all hope.*

Stiles's wife testified to the same information, attesting its truth to Dr. Harris and the court. On November 22, 1906, the jury found the Farlow brothers guilty of giving alcohol to Erma Miller, a minor at the time. They were sentenced to twenty days each in jail.

The power of reputation was much stronger then. It makes one think what would happen if such an accusation were made today. It's heartbreaking to think of how Stiles was so upset that he committed suicide. The *Albany Democrat* was quoted in the *Eugene Weekly* as saying:

> *The Albany friends of J.S. Stiles, Marshal of Eugene, will be glad to know that the reports of immoral conduct made and believed to be the cause of his death were not true. This was brought out in the trial in the circuit court of Virgil Rowland and comes from other sources. Stiles thought he was disgraced from the fact of the warrant being issued and so ended his life. He should have faced the music and established his innocence, but it seems he had been under a physician's care for two years and was discouraged.*

Stiles left behind his wife, Sadie (Klingersmith) Stiles; Edward, the older child from his first marriage, of Portland; four children with Sadie (William, Mabel, Harold and Lloyd); and a stepson, Charles.

On March 16, 1906, the case of Virgil Rowland ended in a split jury trial, with nine jury votes for conviction and three for acquittal. He had vigorously denied all charges of providing alcohol to Ruby and Erma Miller, as well as any hint of a relationship. Witness Edward Bushnell, the owner of the local Meat Market, testified that Ruby Miller and Erma Miller would "hang around" the hopyard adjacent after picking hops and asked him if they could have some money. When he refused, their father came to him and said that "he would take $500.00 to drop the case." Lodging House owner Mrs. Anna Holden swore that she never knew of an occasion when Rowland had "occupied a room together in her lodging house, and if they had done so she would have known it." The lodging house was also in the small residential area nearby the police station. Another jury vote was taken, and the vote was still split, eleven to one. Arrangements were made for another trial on the first date the court was to reconvene in June of that year. It continued to be put off due to Ruby Miller being ill and then disappeared from both newspapers and court dockets.

Ruby and Erma Miller are seldom found mentioned after the trial. There is very little known about their family, other than they worked at the hopyards around Eugene, and the truth of the matter is lost to time.

ELMER AND RACHAEL WAGSTAFF

EXTERMINATING A MARRIAGE

Rachael Wagstaff knew that her tea had been adulterated with something bad.

POISON IN HER TEA

Albany Woman Accuses Husband of Attempted Murder.

HER LIFE IS INSURED

Elmer Wagstaff, the Beneficiary, Is Said to Have Twice Put Arsenic In His Wife's Cup, But She Still Lives.

The story unfolded in the local papers like a radio soap opera. Rumors that Elmer tried to kill Rachael for her life insurance policy were all over the news and were met with vehement denials. Mr. Elmer Wagstaff and Mrs. Rachael LaPorte were married by Reverend J.T. Abbot at the home of the bride in Albany, Oregon, on March 18, 1894. What happened during the time between then and the accusations of attempted murder?

Elmer Wagstaff was a successful carpenter as of 1904, it seems. A news article had a report of Wagstaff becoming injured when the foreman of the job dropped a chisel on his hand, and it caused a gash that required medical care. These types of events were public business when it happened, but only for people of certain stature, as was typical of the time in the United States.

"The Warwick," teacup graphic from advertisement, 1880. *Collection of Karen Watson.*

The same casual nature that was reported about an important businessman's injury was interesting in its treatment of two other individuals on the same page of the paper. One was a Chinese workman. He wasn't even named in the news brief but was disparaged, nonetheless. The brief, written by the editorial staff, is breathtaking in the racism and cruelty that was commonplace then:

A Chinaman working at the Russ House claims to have been held up Sunday night as early as 10 o'clock. Several around saw something going on but thought nothing of it. The man fled and the police attempted to find him but failed. It was probably some kind of anti-Celestial American who wanted to exercise his fingers.

The other example in the same issue of the newspaper shows how the general populace thought about people who were conferred lesser status and how they were treated. The brief is about a completely different woman whose story is unrelated to this case but is illustrative of the powerlessness women had at that time:

Committed to the Asylum.
Mrs. Anna B., wife of T.A. Hall, of Near Roberts Bridge, was brought to Albany this afternoon, and upon complaint of her husband, was committed to the asylum, to which she was taken on the overland by Sheriff White. She has been insanely jealous so much so as to render it unsafe for her to be at large.

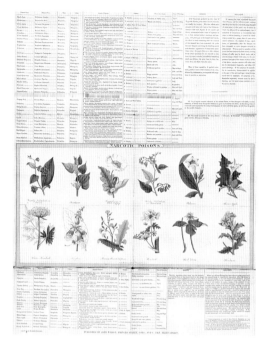

Narcotic poisons botanical drawing, 1902. *Collection of Karen Watson.*

Elmer Wagstaff is mentioned in the newspapers often. Some of the items mention his friendship with one Chas. McKinnon and their fishing trips, as well as Wagstaff being granted a hunting and fishing license. Other articles over several years concerned injuries Wagstaff had on the job.

Wagstaff's trial began on October 25, 1906. Mrs. Rachael Wagstaff testified about the habit she had of preferring cold tea in the mornings. To have that, she was accustomed to brewing the tea the night before and leaving it on the stove until the morning, when she would drink it. At one point in February 1906, she testified that the tea "made her lips pucker" when she tasted the brew and threw the batch away. Her next testimony was most alarming. On the night of March 8, Mrs. Wagstaff was placing a clean handkerchief in her husband's coat pocket when she found a packet of rat poison. Upon recalling the way her tea had tasted before, she grew wary.

The next day, she concealed herself and spied as her husband emptied contents from that package into the tea on the stove:

I saw him walk to the center of the room and stop and seem to meditate for a few minutes. Then he took out the package and poured some in the cup and stirred it with his finger. He walked away but then returned and stirred the tea again with his finger.

Mrs. Rachael Wagstaff then took the tea to Dr. W.H. Davis for testing. She asked her daughter, Pearl La Porte, and friend Vesta Conn to stay the night at their home so she could watch Elmer Flagstaff's behavior the next morning, March 10, 1906. Pearl saw Elmer repeat those actions with the tea that he had taken the day before. They took the second cup for analysis.

When it was found to be poisoned, Elmer Flagstaff was subsequently arrested as he attended a Knights of Pythias club meeting in Scio and held overnight in jail on a $2,500 bond. His motive for poisoning her was said to be the life insurance policy, yes, but after she saw the attempts on her life, Mrs. Rachael Flagstaff "arranged her affairs so that her husband would secure nothing in the event of her death."

In the trial, the first witness was Professor John Fulton, who taught at the Oregon Agricultural College. Fulton spoke of his analysis of the two bottles of tea and said that there were about fourteen grams of arsenic in the bottles—the fumes from said bottles were so strong that he was almost driven from the room. They both contained large quantities of poison, including ground glass, which was one of the things rat poison was made from at the time. Dr. Davis, who worked with Professor Fulton, identified the bottles produced by Fulton as the ones brought to the office for analysis and said that they were brought by Mrs. Rachael Flagstaff.

Then the trial took a different turn. Attorney Percy R. Kelly, for the defense, examined Mrs. Rachael Wagstaff. The marriage, it appeared, had not been a happy one: "Mr. and Mrs. Flagstaff were married twelve years ago. Both have been married before and each have children, and this is said to have caused friction. Mrs. Wagstaff testified that they had not spoken to each other for four months before the alleged attempt at poisoning, any more than was absolutely necessary to live together."

It also came out that she had been the one to initially purchase the arsenic to take care of stray rats and dogs in the area. Elmer Wagstaff's attorney seemed to allude to the idea that she had used it to poison his dog, but it was only mentioned briefly in the accounts, so this may have been false.

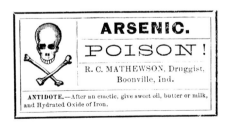

Poison label, 1900. *Collection of Karen Watson.*

Elmer Wagstaff denied any wrongdoing. He said that he had never had or purchased any arsenic or Rough On Rats, as the brand name of the product was called. His defense said that Mrs. Rachael Flagstaff was "erratic" and "insanely jealous." He was written about as "a carpenter" who had "always borne a splendid reputation in Albany." Professor Fulton was brought back to the stand and testified that the tea was "not bitter" or "puckery."

The first jury vote was three for conviction and nine votes to acquit. Elmer Wagstaff's good reputation in the community was seen as a strong point that swayed them in his favor: "'Besides,' remarked a juryman, 'no sane man after he had been discovered in the act charged would have left the poisoned tea where it was sitting on the morning of March 10th.'"

After six hours, the jury returned the verdict: not guilty. The *Corvallis Gazette* ended the news brief, "It is the supposition that the woman [Mrs. Rachael Flagstaff] is not mentally responsible."

On November 2, 1906, the circuit court saw a new case: Elmer Wagstaff against Mrs. Rachael Wagstaff for divorce, citing "cruel and inhumane treatment, fake and wrong accusation of felony followed by arraignment, trial and acquittal." The divorce was granted on November 14, 1906.

JOHNNY BRUNO

DUMPSTER DIVING FOR DEATH

What would you do if you were just looking for dinner and you found what looked like it might be a piece of a person?

A pair of unhoused people discovered a lot of cardboard in the dumpster they looked in at 12:30 a.m. in the early morning of February 24, 1978, near a grocery store in Eugene, Oregon. The store bordered the Millrace, a canal that connected two sloughs near the University of Oregon that was a popular place for people without homes to congregate. Cardboard was what they were looking for. Instead, they found twenty-five- to thirty-pound plastic bags full of a mysterious meat-like substance amid the cardboard. On closer inspection, they were clearly parts of a human being and were covered with teeth marks. The contents were rancid and bloodless, and the two men vomited before racing to the closest pay phone to call the police.

The detective district commander who got the late-night call and his officers worked tirelessly to find clues from the blocked-off dumpster area. Nothing was found, and the searches of nearby dumpsters did not reveal anything either. The search continued.

In a short time, the deputy Lane County medical examiner determined that the remains were part of a human thigh and breast, though so disfigured by bite marks that it was hard to tell. They conducted blood tests to identify the victim. Unfortunately, there was very little blood present to do so. Nonetheless, tests continued.

An article on the mystery appeared in the University of Oregon newspaper, the Springfield newspaper and the *Register-Guard*, the area's largest news

University of Oregon, Deady Hall—near where the body parts of Pamela Bruno were found. The building was established in 1876 in honor of Matthew Deady, Oregon's first federal judge, and renamed University Hall in 2020 due to Deady's racist views. Image dated 1951. *Marion Dean Ross, Library of Congress Prints and Photographs Division.*

outlet. Accounts of missing women were not plentiful exactly, but people did disappear from time to time. Police scoured their missing reports and eventually found two possible victims.

One was a young mother who had been at Sacred Heart General Hospital in downtown Eugene to nurse her premature daughter. Hospital staff saw her leave the hospital at about 11:00 a.m. and exit the parking area. She never showed up to her next destination. Instead, her car and purse were found in separate parking garages in the nearby town of Springfield.

The second missing woman was twenty-five-year-old Pamela Bruno, a housewife who was known to have lived in several dilapidated residences around Eugene and Springfield with her husband, twenty-seven-year-old Johnny, a local tree planter. She had last been seen on February 16, 1978. She wasn't reported missing then, however, but Johnny Bruno did eventually file a report. His explanation left something to be desired: "'This has happened several times in the past, according to Mr. Bruno,' Chief Riley said in the *Register-Guard* article. 'It's not unusual for her to be gone this long.'"

Springfield police chief Brian Riley found that Pamela Bruno, who was known to drink heavily, often visited local taverns and bars and did not drive herself, so she secured rides from other patrons or hitchhiked to get where she was going. She was not usually gone more than two or three days at a time, so this extended absence was unusual. Johnny Bruno further said that Pamela Bruno had left him "eight or nine times previously" to explain his delay in calling in her disappearance.

After a lot of investigative work by both the forensic team from the Oregon State Police Crime Labs and the University of Oregon, they came up with a rough estimate of what the deceased person looked like. They also found that the blood type did not match the young mother who had disappeared from Sacred Heart General Hospital. The search for her and for Pamela Bruno continued while scientists continued to work.

Police found incongruous details when they uncovered Johnny Bruno's record. He had been convicted for driving under the influence of intoxicants and a hit-and-run. He and Pamela Bruno had also been found guilty of contributing to the delinquency of a minor. The minors in question were two fifteen-year-olds to whom he and Pamela had given alcohol, and he later had sex with one or possibly both while Pamela watched.

The police went to the home of the Brunos to search for evidence and to help find Pamela by determining her correct blood type. While there, they asked Johnny Bruno for help, but he was unhelpful—he didn't know her blood type. So, they left with only hair samples.

Sandy Jug Tavern, 1976. *John Margolies, John Margolies Roadside America Photograph Archive (1972–2008), Library of Congress, Prints and Photographs Division.*

The scientists continued to refine their hypotheses as they conducted more tests. With Pamela Bruno's blood type, they were able to find out that hers was a match to the blood type of the tissue found at the crime scene.

A detective from the Springfield Police Department came to notify Johnny Bruno that they thought the victim was likely Pamela, according to the *Eugene Register-Guard*. During the time he was speaking to Mr. Bruno, his dog came in and started to bark loudly. He yelled at it: "'I've got to get rid of that damn dog, too,' Bruno remarked to the detective."

The detective was suspicious. He asked Bruno to imagine what the body parts found in the dumpster looked like. To his surprise, Bruno described them precisely. The investigation confirmed that the body parts did belong to Pamela Bruno. They got warrants for the search of the Bruno residence but were unable to find any evidence that Pamela Bruno had been killed there.

They still had enough to arrest Johnny Bruno for questioning. He did not reveal anything until the detective suggested that he had not acted alone. Then he unleashed the full, grisly story in his confession.

The Bruno couple had hitchhiked into Eugene to the home of fellow tree-planter Charles Haynes and his wife, Lionetti. The group drank and smoked pot together and then engaged in group sex, after which Bruno said Lionetti was jealous and stabbed Pamela first. Then the two men went on to stab Pamela repeatedly, nearly draining her body of blood and dismembering it in the bathtub before dropping it off at various locations. Charles and Lionetti Haynes were arrested and jailed subsequent to their questioning, and evidence was found at their home to corroborate Johnny Bruno's story.

Johnny Charles Bruno's trial started on May 23, 1978. Bruno admitted his part in the murder and the events leading up to it but said that Lionetti was the first to stab Pamela and it was Charles Haynes's idea to dismember Pamela's body. They hung her body above a bathtub at the Haynes home for all the blood to drain from it before it was driven in pieces to separate locations. He indicated that he was afraid of Haynes and claimed that he had been the ringleader in the atrocity.

Others came to the stand to testify against Bruno. A neighbor related how he would kick Pamela with his steel-toes boots and that once he saw Bruno try to throw Pamela at an oncoming car. A psychiatrist testified that he was such an alcoholic the event could have taken place while he was in a blackout state. Despite those and others' accounts both for and against his character, the jury decided Bruno guilty after a short deliberation. He appealed the verdict, but the judgment was upheld. He was sentenced to life in jail and remains there today.

Charles Haynes's trial was scheduled on June 13, 1978. A short time before it was to start, he waived his right to a jury trial. The judge then sentenced him to life. By waiving the right to a jury trial, he did not admit guilt, but instead admitted that there was evidence to convict him. He was therefore able to appeal, which he did, and he received a new trial in Salem in May 1981. His conviction was also upheld, and he was sentenced to life.

Lionetti Haynes had been in jail since her arrest. She had filed a motion that she had been denied a speedy trial, but the judges found that it was due to her continued filings that proceedings were delayed. On March 18, 1982, her conviction stood as ruled, and she was convicted to serve twenty years, with time given for the time she had been jailed awaiting trial.

ELWIN BROWN AND VIRGINIA HARINGTON

LUMBER TOWN LAWBREAKERS

E lwin S. Brown confessed to the robbery as best as he could recollect it. The tiny lumber town crime drama made the biggest newspaper in the state when he was reported in the *Salem Capitol Journal* as saying:

> *He could not remember details of the beating he gave Colegaard. He told authorities he had entered the store, ordered a pair of overalls and a pair of gloves and when the shopkeeper opened the door to get change, stepped around the counter and slugged him.*

The small Elmira, Oregon general store owner Peter Colegaard was helping the young man on March 4, 1937, when Brown jumped over the wooden countertop and beat him severely. It was a dramatic event for the tiny town tucked in the woods of the Willamette Valley between several lumber mills.

While Colegaard was lying on the floor, Brown stole goods and the money from the safe and register. He cleared about $7 (in 2022, that would be about $140). That does not seem like enough to warrant committing such a violent crime, but desperation creates opportunities. Brown fled to the bigger small town of Cottage Grove, about forty miles south. He was arrested there after he had taken a shoe to be repaired. The shoe, which he did not pick up, was said to have matched prints found at the scene.

When he was arrested, Brown said in the *Journal* of the crime that "[h]e could not remember how many times he struck the elderly man before leaving him on the floor, taking the money bag from the safe and throwing his wooden club into the stove to destroy it. He then went back to the cash register, collected a quantity of small change, and fled."

He was then questioned for forty-eight grueling hours about the crime of theft and assault of the seventy-six-year-old Peter Colegaard. Brown remained in the jail with charges pending, depending on whether Colegaard survived. Meanwhile, a strange angle grew in this case. The Eugene police arrested a different man named Joe Elder, charged with drunkenness. To their surprise, he stated to talk about the Elmira robbery case. When the police officers tried to find out more, he abruptly jumped up and yelled that two hours before, he'd taken poison. Then, just as suddenly, he fell to the floor.

They took him immediately to the hospital to have his stomach pumped. There was nothing in his stomach to indicate that he had taken poison. Afterward, he told his strange, rambling story about being part of a gang, noting that the people in the gang were somehow connected to the robbery. When they inquired why he would poison himself, he answered that "he was

Pine Forest, Oregon. Print shows a man measuring the diameter of a large old-growth tree, 1844. *Engraving by W.E. Tucker, drawing by J. Drayton, Library of Congress, Prints and Photographs Division.*

afraid he knew too much" and that for a person who had "as much bad luck and been broken up as much as I have, it didn't matter anyway."

Elder then told the police that he should just "finish what he started if physicians would just give him some strychnine." The police didn't believe his story but kept him in the town jail while the investigation developed. It ended up being a red herring and eventually had no bearing on the case, but the coincidence was enough for police to investigate. He was eventually released.

Colegaard succumbed to his injuries on March 8 after a short window of a possible recovery. He had rallied but never completely regained consciousness. Brown had to be moved from the Eugene jail to the Corvallis jail for safekeeping because officers had heard that a possible lynching might be carried out by Eugene and Elmira residents. He was formally indicted for the murder of Peter Colegaard on March 16, 1937.

The trial began on April 5. It was the first murder trial in Lane County in more than eight years. The attorneys for Brown argued that there were "technical errors in the indictment," but Judge G.F. Skipworth did not agree. Then, on March 22, his attorneys argued that the indictment was invalid because he was charged with "premeditated crimes," while the murder was committed by accident in the act of robbery. Thus, they claimed, he was being charged with two crimes.

On April 11, the verdict was reached. The *Oregon Statesman* put it well: "A month ago, aged Peter P. Colegaard, Elmira shopkeeper, died from a beating. Today, 23-year-old Elwin S. Brown entered the state prison for life." The jury of seven women and five men took twenty minutes to convict Brown of first-degree murder. He was handed a sentence of life in prison and was in the jail two hours later. Judge Skipworth asked Brown if he had any comments. He said, "Nothing except to thank the court and all of you for being fair to me." Judge Skipworth said further that he had never seen a "case conducted with more ability and fairness on both sides" in the twenty-two years he had been on the bench.

The tragic story of Virginia and Gene Harington is another lumber town tale. On January 28, 1947, lumber magnate Gene Harington, thirty-three, was shot to death by his "pert young wife." The operator of two lumber mills was found in a pool of blood, in his bed, on the morning of the twenty-eighth in the couple's "fashionable home on College Hill."

His wife, Virginia Harington, twenty-three, was the one who called the police. "Send someone out right away," she said. She further told them that her husband, Gene, had "come home drunk about 5:30 Tuesday morning

Long-Bell Lumber Company, located in Vaughn, Oregon, dated August 1947. *Kenrossalex, Rosboro Lumber Company.*

and started an argument, during which he threatened to kill her. After a two-and-a-half-hour quarrel, she related, she snatched the 38-caliber pistol from him and fired a shot."

The Eugene coroner said that Harington died after being struck by two bullets in the face. They were so deep into the pillow that he estimated they were fired from a distance of about two feet away. The Eugene district attorney, Edward Luckey, said the evidence further showed that the bedding was pulled tight around him, as if he had tucked himself in, and not askew, as it would have been in the event of a violent argument. The coroner did say that Gene Harington was "a little intoxicated" and that his blood alcohol level was about .017 percent.

The Harington couple had two children: a two-year-old son and an eighteen-month-old daughter. The children were moved to a "welfare home," and Virginia Harington was held in the Lane County Jail without bail. She was to wait there for a grand jury meeting; her parents, Mr. and Mrs. Anthony Reggio, arrived from San Jose, California.

In an article for *OregonLive*, the online journal for the *Oregonian*, the trial was likened to the musical *Chicago*: a beautiful young wife—almost every news article and outlet mentioned both qualities—on trial for murdering her husband. Photos of her looking composed, put together and innocent helped bolster that view.

Gene Harington had told Virginia that he was working late at one of his properties with his secretary and then driving around late on the night

This page: Sawmill near Mapleton, 1936. *Arthur Rothstein, Farm Security Administration— Office of War Information Photograph Collection, Library of Congress.*

Top: Willamette Valley—part of a photo serries chronicling the American people, 1939. *Dorothea Lange, Farm Security Administration.*

Bottom: Oregon barn, 1942. *Russell Lee, Library of Congress, Prints and Photographs Division.*

before the shooting. At 3:00 a.m. the night before, he was heard arguing with Virginia while on the phone by a night watchman and gave him the phone to prove to Virginia that he wasn't "with a woman."

During the trial, which started on March 12, Virginia Harington "told a circuit court that she shot her husband last January 28 out of fear for herself and her children." Her defense portrayed Gene Harington as a man who drank heavily and was subject to frequent fits of rage. She said that he

Cleaver home at the end of the dusty road in lonely rural Oregon, 1939. *Dorothea Lange, Farm Security Administration—Office of War Information Photograph Collection, Library of Congress.*

was prone to hitting and kicking her when he was angry. The prosecution had earlier claimed that Gene Harington was shot while he was sleeping, countering her claims of a fight.

The nine-man, three-woman jury, selected to be "beauty proof," were told on March 14 during the final arguments phase of the trial that they could choose to "find Mrs. Harington guilty as charged, in which case [a] life sentence would be mandatory; or they might judge her guilty of manslaughter; or they might acquit her."

The truth of the matter is a mystery. The verdict of the jury was given on March 15 at 1:30 p.m.: Virginia Harington was acquitted. The *Oregonian* reported, "Mrs. Harington's only reaction was a single audible sob….Later, however, amid congratulating friends, she broke down and cried."

NATURAL DISASTERS

WHEN THE DANGER COMES FROM OUTSIDE

The terrain of the Pacific Northwest is primed for the "Big One," an enormous earthquake of unprecedented proportions. Such an event would likely shut off communications, stop water and electricity to homes and generally disrupt and halt emergency medical services.

The first recorded instance of major historic events occurred about one thousand years ago at the top of a valley. From a scientific perspective, it is explained that the Columbia River, about forty miles east of Portland, became blocked by a huge mudslide, the Bonneville Landslide. The blockage made parts of the inland area of Oregon, Washington and Idaho an enormous lake. The natural barrier wore away in part over the years and made a natural bridge. As the bridge itself corroded and fell, the Cascade Rapids were formed.

The Washington State Department of Natural Resources, located just across the border, noted:

> Hundreds of years ago, an entire hillside along the Columbia River collapsed in a massive landslide covering an area of about six square miles. The Bonneville landslide was so huge that it created a natural dam in the Columbia River, forming a temporary lake stretching all the way to Wallula Gap, 150 miles upriver. The deposit is known as the "Bridge of the Gods" because it temporarily connected the land on both sides of the Columbia River. The modern-day bridge at Cascade Locks is named after this prehistoric land bridge.

The Bridge of the Gods is a steel truss cantilever bridge that spans the Columbia River between Cascade Locks, Oregon, and Washington State near North Bonneville. It was completed by the Wauna Toll Bridge Company and opened in 1926 at a length of 1,127 feet. Image dated 2017. *Steven Pavlov.*

The Bonneville landslide's headscarp is exposed on Table Mountain, which has an almost vertical 800-foot-tall open face close to its peak. Table Mountain is composed of Columbia River Basalt (CRB) lava flows, that sit on top of the sedimentary Eagle Creek Formation. The sedimentary rock weathers into clay as water trickles down through cracks in the CRB lavas. The Bonneville landslide, like many of the large landslides in the Cascade landslide complex, was activated when CRBs slid along this weak clay layer.

The Native American tribes of the area, the Cascades and Chinook, fished the river. One legend of the bridge's formation starts with the great spirit Manito creating a land bridge to help the people cross. They were afraid that the bridge would wash out. After they came to him with their concerns, Manito appointed a guardian woman called Loo-Wit to stand watch. He also sent his sons: Klickitat, now known as Mount Adams; Multnomah, known as Mount Rainier; and Wyeast, known as Mount Hood. They all existed peacefully together. One day, the Squaw Mountain settled in between Klickitat and Wyeast. The brothers became jealous of the attention she paid the other and began to fight, throwing rocks and fireballs, "[s]etting fire to the forests and driving the people into hiding. Finally, they threw so many stones onto the Bridge of the Gods and shook the earth so hard that the stone bridge broke in the middle and fell in the river."

The fight angered Manito greatly, and he formed the rapids as a result. Klickitat and Wyeast ended their battle, with Klickitat as the winner. Squaw Mountain, whose heart belonged to Wyeast, had to move toward Wyeast and slumped in defeat on the Mount Adams/Klickitat side, now referred to as Sleeping Beauty Peak. Klickitat also bent the top of his mountain in sorrow. Loo-Wit, who had tried to mediate between the brothers to stop the fight, was unsuccessful and the bridge collapsed. Manito learned of her loyalty and offered to give her one wish. Although she was old, she wished for youth and beauty but also for solitude. Manito made her the youngest mountain in the cascades, Mount St. Helens.

Both the scientific and legendary explanations of the fall of the Bridge of the Gods are fascinating, but the enormous impact the bridge's collapse had on the land created the Cascade rapids and changed the way the water flowed through the valleys via the Columbia and, farther south, the Willamette River.

THE VANPORT FLOODS OF May 1942 were a senseless tragedy. KOIN-TV reported on the seventy-third anniversary of the flood:

> *Vanport was once Oregon's second largest city built in 1942 to accommodate Black and poor shipyard workers moving to the greater Portland area during World War II. At its peak, it housed 40,000, and became the country's largest housing project at the time.*

The predominantly Black area near of Portland was about twenty thousand people strong. It was made up of middle- and working-class Americans, many employed in the shipyards of the area. The human impact is hard to overestimate. It was a diaspora of those who had built their lives there and intended to keep on doing so. A history article on "Black Past," by Rudy Pearson, said of the time:

> *The first black teachers and policemen in the state were hired in Vanport during the war years. The Vanport Interracial Council worked to establish a Portland office of the Urban League. Vanport College was the precursor to Portland State University where many veterans used the GI Bill to get a new start on life.*

Local officials gave notice of possible danger, but it was downplayed. May 30, 1942, saw a flyer slipped under the doors of residents that read:

> *REMEMBER.*
> *DIKES ARE SAFE AT PRESENT.*
> *YOU WILL BE WARNED IF NECESSARY.*
> *YOU WILL HAVE TIME TO LEAVE.*
> *DON'T GET EXCITED.*

Besides being misleading, the flyer was too little, too late for what was the second-largest city in Oregon. Governmental agencies and the Vanport College had already moved equipment out of harm's reach but still told the residents "Don't Get Excited." That callous disregard seems criminal today. With little warning, the railroad dike that protected the area from the Columbia became overwhelmed with the snowmelt and was destroyed. There was only one road out of town. Evacuation was necessarily complicated, and the entire town became engulfed in about fifteen feet of water in about two hours. Fifteen people died, and the entire area was erased as the residents in the mainly segregated area had to disperse.

Home Forward, the Portland Housing Authority organization that oversaw the area, admitted "the mishandling of their flood response" decades later. The nearly 6,500 Black residents were forced into the heavily segregated Portland neighborhoods, mainly the Alberta District, which did not offer nearly enough housing. Its residents assimilated into the North Portland neighborhoods, possibly hastening the destruction of de facto segregation in the area, but the destruction of the cultural center had an immense impact.

The Columbus Day Storm in 1962 was the biggest storm the area had seen in recent memory. It was possibly the biggest cyclone not located in a tropical area ever to occur in the United States. It is the state's biggest natural disaster in monetary and physical terms in the twentieth century. The stereotype is that Oregon is one of the country's wettest and rainiest places. That is true; however, when the Columbus Day storm hit the shore in Red Bluff, California, it rained almost a half inch in five minutes and almost an inch in fifteen minutes. The rate, Wolf Read reported, increased to more than eight inches per hour in the first hour that the storm hit. The weather continued up the coast until it had cut a swath from the west that has thankfully never been repeated to such a degree.

In October 1962, a tropical storm that was later called Typhoon Freda formed in the mid-Pacific. The "Big Blow," as it is known, was an enormous storm—one that nobody was ready for. The storm was one of the worst ever to hit North America, even worse than the Halloween nor'easter weather event written about in the book/movie *A Perfect Storm*. Ships at sea on the West Coast had very little warning. "I spent three years at sea," John Hubbard, a deckhand on the USS *Tracer*, stationed off the coast of Northern California, was reported as saying in an article for the *Daily Astorian*, "and that was the worst storm we ever had."

On Friday, October 12, 1962, the storm came ashore as Freda off Northern California, off the coast of Crescent City, and moved north and east at the

The Circuit Rider on the capitol grounds in Salem. The statue was sculpted by A. Phimister Proctor to honor Oregon's circuit-riding ministers. It was presented to the state as a gift in 1924 by Robert A. Booth of Eugene, whose father was a Methodist Episcopal circuit rider. The statue was knocked from its base in the Columbus Day Storm of October 1962. The photo is from the Hugh Stryker Collection, 2003. *Salem Public Library Historic Photograph Collections, Salem Public Library, Salem, Oregon.*

speed of a Category 3 hurricane all the way up to British Columbia in Canada. It measured speeds up to 145 miles per hour. Researchers think that it is possible that the wind speeds reached up to 179 miles per hour, but Cape Blanco, on Oregon's coast, only measured up to 145 at its Coast Guard station.

The barometric pressure dropped abruptly on October 12. In some areas, like Eugene, Oregon, the barometric pressure dropped so low that it fell off the ranges of the chart measuring it, to the extent that it required a new metric on their chart. Enormous damage ensued as roofs were pulled off schools and homes, miles and miles of trees were downed and torrential mudslides occurred, hitting thousands of buildings and downing power lines. The Oregon Encyclopedia said of the severity, "The intense winds left over a million people in Oregon without electrical power, some of them for weeks."

John Dodge reported in an article for "What It Means to Be an American, A National Conversation" that Steve Pierce, president of the Oregon Chapter of the American Meteorological Society, said, "There has yet to be another tempest that even comes close to the furor of the Columbus Day Storm."

The storm destroyed a U.S. Air Force radar station on Mount Hebo. The 1962 World Series game between the New York Yankees and the San Francisco Giants had to be postponed. It knocked a bronze statue off its pedestal in Salem, Oregon. The number of homes standing in Lake Oswego, Oregon, was reduced by 70 percent after the storm. The 1962 World's Fair, occurring in Seattle at the time, was in the last week of its seven-month run. The wave-like movement of the Space Needle on October 12 was frightening enough for the building to be cleared. In the Willamette Valley, so many of the fruit and nut orchards were destroyed that it made way for the creation of the now world-renowned wine industry when the owners needed to restart. It was said that it was more unusual for a home in the storm's path to be undamaged than damaged after the huge storm.

In an article for the University of Washington, author Wolf Read wrote about the observation report from the site of the Corvallis, Oregon weather station that day:

> *Winds at 16:00 had elevated to 60 knots gusting to 85 (69 mph gusting to 98), with a peak gust noted at 110 knots (127 mph)! Just a few moments later, at 16:15, "ABANDONED STATION" is clearly written in the middle of the form. The next day, it is also noted, "Unreported from 04:00—12:00 due power failure and instruments demolished." This is the only time in the history of the Pacific Northwest that an officially supervised weather station had to be abandoned due to high winds. A strong reminder of just how powerful the Columbus Day Storm was.*

Left: Cape Creek Bridge, Florence, Oregon, 2022. *Photo by author.*

Opposite: Sunset on the Rocky Oregon Coast, 1980. *Carol Highsmith, Photographs in the Carol M. Highsmith Archive, Library of Congress, Prints and Photographs Division.*

In human terms, thirty-eight lives were lost during the storm—most of these from debris or landslide. Scores of loggers, cutting timber in the forest, had to take cover in recently cleared areas to avoid tree falls. Power was out for two to three weeks in areas. Estimates are that more than $800 million of damage was incurred (in 2022 dollars). More than fifty thousand homes and buildings were lost, and countless livestock were killed by debris, power lines or flood.

The Western Regional Climate Center stated, "In fact, the amount of trees blown down during the Columbus Day storm was nearly 15 times that blown down by the 1980 eruption of Mount St. Helens."

JOHN ACKROYD

HEINOUS EVENTS ON HIGHWAY 20

This killer, though lesser known than some of the state's serial killers, haunted the roads of Oregon for several decades before he was caught. His swath of horror cut across the state and the Willamette Valley. Highway 20 goes on a rural route from Newport on the coast, around and through the small towns of Lebanon, Sweet Home, Santiam Junction, Sisters and Bend to enter the Cascade Mountains.

Kaye Turner was the first to disappear. She had set out for a long run from where she and her husband were camping in Camp Sherman around 8:15 in the morning, according to reporter Kate Seamons from Newser.com. She had not yet returned by ten o'clock, and her husband grew worried. He called the police.

Noelle Crombie wrote that a state highway mechanic, John Ackroyd, was the early frontrunner as a suspect. The police were already aware of Ackroyd and the fact that he had been accused of raping Marlene Gabrielson a year before. Police had decided not to press charges regarding the rape. When questioned about Turner, Ackroyd told the police that he had seen Turner running, but they decided to focus on other details instead; the police investigation ended up centering on Turner's two extramarital affairs. The investigation went on.

The woman who ran the Camp Sherman store was surprised when, eight months later, John Ackroyd came into the counter and told her that he'd found what looked like parts of a human skeleton while rabbit hunting. She was understandably freaked out and got her husband, who also helped run the store, to call the state police.

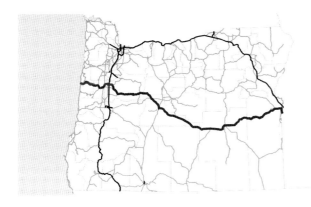

Oregon U.S. Route 20 is the highway in red that bisects the state horizontally. You can also see the Willamette River, the vertical line, and the Columbia River, the horizontal line, on this map, 2008. *NE2, Oregon Department of Transportation.*

John Ackroyd was, incredibly, able to bring the police to the site where he found the remains, as Holly M. Gill reported in the *Madras Pioneer*: "In a macabre twist, in August of 1979 he led searchers to an area where he claimed have found human remains while walking his dog."

It looked like a big pile of trash with bone mixed in. The police team found a jawbone and assorted clothing, which included a Nike running shoe and the watch Turner was known to wear, broken. Another policeman looked up to see what looked like some blond hair in the structure of a bird's nest.

Police grew more wary of John Ackroyd when he changed his story. Originally, he'd told them he had seen Turner running. Now he said he had talked to her. He also changed his story to admit that he had seen the remains months before and even touched them. His last revelation was that he had been with his friend Roger Dale Beck the morning that Turner had vanished. They were not hunting for rabbits (which would have been unusual for that time of year)—they had been illegally hunting for deer.

After a long period in the outdoors, no physical evidence linked Ackroyd or Beck to the body. It had withstood enough exposure, and the body had been in such a rustic area that the investigation petered out. Eventually, they let it go, and Ackroyd and Beck went back to their lives. Ackroyd worked for the state and cleaned up car accidents, fixed state-owned cars and went on calls when vehicles broke down.

He married Linda Pickle, a woman who had two kids, Rachanda and Byron. They made a life for themselves in the area as one of about twelve or thirteen families around. Their relationship was quite unusual in that they divorced after close to a year but chose to remain living together as married people in every other way. His friend Roger Beck committed sexual assault in the state of Minnesota and was jailed there for seven months before he moved to California.

Postcard advertising the "Metola Rest" campground, Camp Sherman, as viewed from the Metolius River. Image is assumed to date to the 1940s, when the campground area was constructed. *Gerald W. Williams Collection, OSU Special Collections & Archives.*

Noelle Crombie wrote, "Kaye Turner's killing became a faded memory," and it did. People also forgot about John Ackroyd until his thirteen-year-old stepdaughter, Rachanda Pickle, vanished. Rachanda, called "Channy" for short, was alone at their house at Santiam Junction. Santiam Junction is the major turning point from the Eugene/Springfield area, and it is a large, red cinder-dusted compound. The cinder is collected in big piles there to dust on the roads to aid with traction in the ice and snow that often builds up on the sides of the roads in winter. The compound looks like a forestry station, not a place where a manufactured home would nestle up to the forest, as their home did.

She was there without her brother, older by one year, because he had chosen to stay at their father Steven Pickle's home for their scheduled visit time, while she returned home, homesick. Thirteen-year-old Rachanda was extremely close to her mother, Linda. She didn't love being in the woods and generally preferred to go roam outside when her brother was around.

After Linda woke Rachanda that day, her daughter braided her hair, and then Linda Pickle had John drop her off at Black Butte Resort, where she worked as a housekeeper. John checked in with his job and then decided to

Snowplows clear U.S. 20. One of the jobs John Ackroyd did while he was working on the highway, 2014. *Oregon Department of Transportation.*

take the day off. When he got home, he claimed that he saw Rachanda on the couch, and when he asked her to go take photos of deer, she declined. Instead of going with her stepfather on the day she disappeared, he said that she decided to stay home and watch cartoons in her pajamas.

He left to go to work and then pick up Linda, and when he and his wife got back, Rachanda was gone. Her chores looked undone. Her things were still there, but Rachanda was not. John told his wife to wait until the morning to call her in missing. The next morning, Linda called 911. The police arrived fast and made a connection with John and Kaye Turner. John Ackroyd denied any involvement with either disappearance.

Then the police, looking at evidence from the Turner investigation, made another pass at the information on Roger Dale Beck. He had been married at the time Turner disappeared, and his wife gave both men an alibi.

Officer Will McAnulty thought to drive to California and interview Beck's ex-wife to check out the alibi. In the interview, his wife, "who had been Ackroyd's high school sweetheart and divorced Beck in 1985," changed her story. Both men had told her to lie. They had come in from "hunting" in blood-soaked clothing and said that they had thought Turner was a deer, so they accidently shot her. After a time, Beck told her the truth, which was that they had raped and shot her.

Investigators kept looking at Ackroyd, who had broken up with his wife, Rachanda's mother. He moved in with his mother in Sweet Home and was transferred from Santiam Junction but kept working out of Corvallis. He was driving with a friend, who introduced him to Melissa Sanders, seventeen, and Sheila Swanson, nineteen. The two were part of a group that hung around the local Shari's.

Scene along Suttle Lake, with view of Black Butte in the Cascade Mountains. Ackroyd prowled these hills and hunted along the roads nearby. Because he never confessed, we may never know if there more of his victims in these hills, 2018. *Carol M. Highsmith Archive, Library of Congress.*

The girls continued to be friendly with Ackroyd. The pair were camping with family at Beverly Beach State Park. Somewhere on a lonely mountain road, they were thought to have met with Ackroyd. They disappeared. "On Oct. 10, hunters found their bodies 20 miles east of Newport near Eddyville about 50 feet from a logging road in thick brush," one source read. A rivet and beads from a beaded seat cover were found, but that's all. The conclusion that investigators came to was that the two girls had left their campsites in the early morning, possibly to meet up with their boyfriends or to hitchhike home.

A few weeks after the girls disappeared, in 1992, Ackroyd was arrested on suspicion of the death of Kaye Turner. Forensic testing had finally caught up to the case, and it was being worked by new investigators. Investigators uncovered allegations that he had been sexually and physically abusing Rachanda Pickle as well. He was tried in court. The trial presented fiber, blood and testimony, including testimony from a woman who had been involved in a confrontation with Ackroyd that eerily echoed the day Kaye Turner disappeared. Ackroyd accosted her as she was riding her bike early in the day and pointed a handgun at her. The woman followed her instinct to bike away as fast as she could, and it probably saved her life. It was a detail that must have impressed the jury because according to Crombie's article for *OregonLive*, "It took the jury just four hours. Guilty." He got a life sentence.

Evidence uncovered by the tireless investigators, as reported in the *Ghosts of Highway 20* documentary and various newspapers, was scant. But interviews with the survivors, including the original rape victim Marlene K. Gabrielson, and circumstantial evidence, along with Beck and Ackroyd's contradictory statements, were enough to swing the verdict against Ackroyd.

His hunting buddy and accomplice Roger Dale Beck was found guilty of murder and sentenced to life in a different trial. Beck later appealed the decision in 2013 and 2015, saying that he had been hunting and drinking with Ackroyd that night but that the blood on his person was from a deer they had skinned. He further maintained that the people testifying against him were the ones not telling the truth. District Attorney Steve Leriche said of Beck after reading the appeal and trial case files, "It would seem that nothing has substantially changed," with Beck's behavior.

A woman named Elizabeth Mussler was buried alongside Highway 20. Two other unidentified women were found dead on Highway 20. All are thought to be his victims.

Despite an immense amount of work by police and investigators, including "an extensive search in the area of Hoodoo, Potato Hill and Lost Lake," Rachanda has never been found. Ackroyd died in prison on December 30, 2016, without telling the truth about just whom he killed and when. He left no note or confession.

BIBLIOGRAPHY

Abraham, Nehita. "Jerry Brudos: The Making of the 'Shoe Fetish Slayer.'" *Daily Hawker*, March 18, 2020. https://www.dailyhawker.com/articles/jerry-brudos.

Albany Daily Democrat. "Married." March 19, 1894, 3.

Albany Democrat. August 12, 1904, 7.

———. "Circuit Court." November 2, 1906, 4.

———. "Committed to the Asylum." August 12, 1904, 7.

———. "Elmer Wagstaff Not Guilty." October 26, 1906, 7.

Alchetron. "Edmund Creffield." May 19, 2018. https://alchetron.com/Edmund-Creffield.

Appeal from the Circuit Court of the Second Circuit. No. 17601. Intermediate Court of Appeals, March 11, 2003.

Atwood, Kay, and Dennis J. Gray. "Claiming The Land." The Oregon History Project, 2003, 2017. https://www.oregonhistoryproject.org/articles/claiming-the-land/#.Y3QTUHbMK70

Biography. "Jerome Brudos Biography." April 2, 2014. https://www.biography.com/crime-figure/jerome-brudos.

Black, Adrian. "Between Two Noirs." *Ethos*, September 24, 2012.

Capitol Journal. "Brown Trial Set for Monday." March 31, 1937, 9.

———. "Governor Offers Reward for Killer." September 16, 1930, 4.

———. "Harington Case to Reach Jury Today." March 14, 1947, 11.

———. "Woman Says Murder Induced by Fear." March 13, 1947, 11.

Christensen, Tricia. "How Has the Average Age at Marriage Changed Over Time?" Cultural World, May 2, 2022. https://www.culturalworld. org/how-has-the-average-age-at-marriage-changed-over-time.htm.

Coe, Daniel E. "Bonneville Landslide, Bridge of the Gods." *Washington Geological Survey*. Fort Rains: Washington State Department of Natural Resources, April 22, 2021.

The Columbian. "Authorities ID Another Alleged Victim of Molalla Forest Killer." November 13, 2013.

Cooley, Michael F., and Mary Lou Cooley. *The Transcribed Diary of Eli Casey Cooley.* http://oregonpioneers.com/CooleyDiary.htm#:~:text=An%20 estimated%203000%20emigrants%20traveled%20over%20the%20 Oregon,have%20doubled%20the%20non-Indian%20population%20 of%20the%20territory.

Cornelius, Jim. "Killer of Camp Sherman Jogger Dies in Prison." *The Nugget*, January 4, 2017, 17.

Corvallis Gazette. "Prof. Fulton a Witness." October 26, 1906, 1.

Corvallis Times. "In Benton Again—But Only Passed Through—Creffield, the Monster—More Rollerism." April 24, 1906, 2.

———. "Their Queer Acts." October 31, 1903, 2.

Crombie, Noelle. "*Oregonian/OregonLive* Fought to Unseal Secret Deal in Rachanda Pickle's Killing." *OregonLive*, December 7, 2018. https://www. oregonlive.com/news/2018/12/oregonianoregonlive-fought-to-unseal-secret-deal-in-rachanda-pickles-killing.html.

Daily Capitol Journal. "Declared Insane." March 20, 1897, 4.

———. "Joseph Stiles." March 9, 1906, 1.

Dodge, John. "The Long, Violent 1962 Storm that Inspired the Environmental Movement." What It Means to Be American, 2019. https://www.whatitmeanstobeamerican.org/places/the-long-violent-1962-storm-that-inspired-the-environmental-movement.

Edwards, Pat. *From Sawdust & Cider to Wine: A History of Lorane, Oregon & the Siuslaw Valley*. Lorane, OR: Groundwaters Publishing, 2012.

Encyclopedia.com. "Charity Lamb Trial: 1854." https://www. encyclopedia.com/law/law-magazines/charity-lamb-trial-1854.

Eugene Weekly Guard. "Brevities." March 16, 1906, 4.

———. "Defense Offers Its Testimony." March 16, 1906, 5.

———. "Farlow Boys Brought Back to Eugene." March 16, 1906, 7.

———. "Jury Still Out." November 22, 1906, 4.

———. "Note and Comment." March 16, 1906, 7.

———. "Stiles Takes His Own Life." March 16, 1906, 7.

Evening Herald. "The End of a Criminal." November 28, 1930, 4.

FirstPeople. "Bridge of the Gods." https://www.firstpeople.us/FP-Html-Legends/The_Bridge_Of_The_Gods-Unknown.html.

Frasier, D.K. *Murder Cases of the Twentieth Century.* Jefferson, NC: McFarland & Company, 1996.

Geiling, Natasha. "How Oregon's Second Largest City Vanished in a Day." *Smithsonian Magazine* (February 18, 2015). https://www.smithsonianmag.com/history/vanport-oregon-how-countrys-largest-housing-project-vanished-day-180954040/#:~:text=Though%20the%20Columbia%20Slough%20succeeded,and%20roughly%206%2C300%20were%20black.

George Grantham Bain Collection, Library of Congress. "O.H. Kelley." Bain News Service, September 24, 2021.

Gill, Holly M. "Infamous Murderer Dies in Prison." *Madras Pioneer,* January 4, 2017. https://pamplinmedia.com/msp/129-news/338768-218610-infamous-murderer-dies-in-prison.

Golembo, Max. "What Is a Typhoon." *ABC News,* July 12, 2018. https://abcnews.go.com/US/typhoon-/story?id=56540857.

Grunbaum, Mara. "The Story Behind the Lone Fir Cemetery." *Street Roots,* November 27, 2008.

Holes, Paul. *Unmasked.* New York: Macmillan, 2022.

Hood, Washington, cartographer. *Map of the United States, Territory of Oregon, West of the Rocky Mountains : Exhibiting the Various Trading Depots or Forts Occupied by the British Hudson Bay Company, Connected with the Western and Northwestern Fur Trade.* Washington, D.C., 1838, reprint 1871. https://www.loc.gov/item/2018588047.

Idaho State Journal. "Hand-Dug Caves." April 23, 1975, 37.

Inflation Calculator. https://www.in2013dollars.com/us/inflation/1937?amount=1.

IPUMS USA. U.S. Census Data for Social, Economic, October 17, 2017. https://usa.ipums.org/usa.

IWSMT. McDonald's menu, 1972. https://iwastesomuchtime.com/91025.

John, Finn J.D. "Ax Murderess Charity Lamb: The Rest of the Story." *Offbeat Oregon,* November 29, 2015. https://offbeatoregon.com/1511e.charity-lamb-murder-367.html.

———. "Oregon's First Murder Defendant Was Saved from the Gallows by His Wife." *Offbeat Oregon,* December 19, 2019. https://www.redmondspokesman.com/features/offbeat-oregon-oregon-s-first-murder-defendant-was-saved-from-gallows-by-his-wife/article_ba508198-2452-11ea-ad12-f3b07f34f0a6.html.

King, Gary C. *Blood Lust: Portrait of a Serial Sex Killer.* N.p.: Bleak House Publishing Inc., 2011.

Koffman, Rebecca. "Planning a Garden for Forgotten Residents." *Oregonian,* October 23, 2008, 8

Krajicek, David J. "The Abused Wife Defense." *New York Daily News,* October 2009. https://www.nydailynews.com/news/crime/abused-wife-defense-article-1.379840.

LaLande, Jeff. "Columbus Day Storm (1962)." *Oregon Encyclopedia,* March 23, 2022. https://www.oregonencyclopedia.org/articles/columbus_day_storm_1962_/#.Yn5SMejMK70.

Lane County. "Hall of Honor—In Memorium." 2016. https://www.lanecounty.org/cms/One.aspx?portalId=3585881&pageId=4252793.

Lansing, Ronald B. "Charity Lamb Trial: 1854." Law Library—American Law and Legal Information. https://law.jrank.org/pages/2532/Charity-Lamb-Trial-1854-Defense-Insanity.html.

———. *Washington State University Press.* July 1, 2005. https://wsupress.wsu.edu/product/nimrod/#:~:text=Ronald%20B.%20Lansing%20%2419.95%20In%201852%2C%2072-year-old%20Nimrod,look%20at%20life%20and%20law%20on%20the%20frontier.

Lebanon Express. "A Woman Shoots Another." October 4, 1895, 1.

Lewis Hartley (Plaintiff) v. Cora A. Hartley (Defendant). No. 4377, Circuit Court of the State of Oregon for Benton County, May 11, 1906.

Lohr, David. "Dayton Leroy Rogers, Serial Killer with Bizarre Foot Fetish, Could Escape Execution." January 3, 2012. https://www.huffpost.com/entry/dayton-leroy-rogers_n_1181287.

Mack, Don. "Husband, Friends Accused of 'Thigh Murder.'" *Register-Guard,* March 13, 1978, 1.

MacNary, Lawrence A. "Oregon's First Reported Murder Case." *Oregon Historical Quarterly* 36, no. 4 (December 1935): 359–64.

McClann, K.M. "The Sun Don't Shine on a Moonshine Still." The Airship. http://airshipdaily.com/moonshine.

McKenzie History Highway. "Nimrod: MILEPOST 35." https://mckenziehistoryhwy.org/settlements/nimrod.

Meeker, Richard H. "Eugene Jails 'Family.'" *Willamette Week,* May 18, 1975, 4.

Morning Oregonian. "Dies in Disgrace." *Morning Oregonian,* March 16, 1906, 6.

———. "In Fear of His Life." May 3, 1906, 6.

———. "Poison in Her Tea." March 14, 1906, 11.

———. "Slayer's Sister Carried Messenges." May 8, 1906, 6.

Net Lawman. "Injunctions: Types and Uses." Suffolk, 2003.

Newton, Michael. "Rogers, Dayton Leroy." An Encyclopedia of Modern Serial Killers, 1988. https://murderpedia.org/male.R/r/rogers-dayton-leroy.htm.

Norman, V.F. "Snake Brooks, Belinda and the Death of Roy Dirks." *One Dollar Magazine* (February 1976): 19–27.

Odeneal, T.B. "Third Generation." The O'Kelley Name, August 1, 1886. http://www.okelley.net/b404.htm.

Oregon-California Trails Association. "Oregon Trail Diaries." 2018. https://octa-trails.org/articles/oregon-trail-diaries.

Oregon Daily Emerald. "Eugene Housewife Held." January 29, 1947, 8.

———. "Police Hold Brooks in Murder Case." April 18, 1975, 2.

Oregon Daily Journal. "Creffield Poses as Jeremiah." May 2, 1906, 4.

———. "Holy Rollers' in Hobo Camp Life." February 1, 1904, 8.

The Oregon History Project. "Claiming the Land." https://www.oregonhistoryproject.org/narratives/as-long-as-the-world-goes-on-the-land-and-people-of-southwest-oregon/new-names-on-the-land/claiming-the-land/#.YU5vvJrMK70.

The Oregonian. Oregon Hospital ad. September 3, 1859.

Oregonian/OregonLive. "Dayton Leroy Rogers Out of Court 40 Years." October 11, 2012.

———. "Detective at Dayton Rogers…Trial." January 9, 2019.

Oregon Statesman. "Colegaard Slayer Handed Life Term." April 11, 1937, 3.

———. "Demurrer Delays." March 23, 1937, 10.

———. "Indict Brown." March 17, 1937, 1.

———. "Old Wounds Found." November 27, 1930, 1.

———. "Posse Shoots Sutherland in Woods." November 26, 1930, 1.

———. "Slain Husband a Little Intoxicated." January 30, 1947 1.

Palombo, Lynne, Kathleen Glanville, Margaret Haberman and Tony Hernandez, comps. "Oregon Death Row." *OregonLive*. https://www.oregonlive.com/pacific-northwest-news/page/oregon_death_row.html.

Paris, Anne Jennings. *Killing George Washington: The American West in Five Voices*. N.p.: Ooligan Press, 2009.

Pearson, Rudy. "Vanport, Oregon (1942–1948)." *BlackPast*, January 22, 2007. https://www.blackpast.org/african-american-history/vanport-1942-1948.

Perry, Douglas. "The Most Cold-Blooded, Cowardly Treachery." *OregonLive*, January 22, 2018. https://www.oregonlive.com/history/2018/01/the_most_cold-blooded_cowardly.html.

Peterson, Danny. "Vanport Flood Survivor: City's Apology 'Meaningless' Without Reparations." KOIN-TV, Portland, June 5, 2021. https://www.koin.com/news/civic-affairs/vanport-flood-survivor-citys-apology-meaningless-without-reparations/#;~:text=But%20a%20survivor%20of%20the%20flood%2C%20artist%20Isaka,notice%20of%20evacuation%20or%20help%20securing%20housing%20afterwards.

Phillips, Rosemary Gartner, and Jim Phillips. "The Creffield-Mitchell Case, Seattle, 1906: The Unwritten Law in the Pacific Northwest." *Pacific Northwest Quarterly* (2003): 69–82.

Port of Cascade Locks. "Bridge of the Gods." 2018. https://portofcascadelocks.org/bridge-of-the-gods.

Read, Wolf. "The 1962 Columbus Day Storm." *Washington Climate*, October 17, 2015. https://climate.washington.edu/stormking/October1962.html.

Reddit. "What Cults Are in Eugene." December 28, 2017. https://www.reddit.com/r/Eugene/comments/7mgdln/what_cults_are_in_eugene.

Reeves, Carol. "Exploring the Cult of Corvallis." *Corvallis Gazette-Times*, May 20, 2002.

Roseburg News-Review. "Confession of Deed Made by Elwin Brown." March 5, 1937, 1–3.

———. "Deputies Shot Down." August 29, 1930, 1, 6.

———. "Elmira Slugger Jailed in Eugene." March 5, 1937, 3.

———. "Sutherland's Son." September 12, 1930, 1.

Ruggles, Steven. *The Rise of Divorce and Separation in the United States, 1880–1990.* Bethesda, MD: U.S. National Libraries of Medicine, National Institutes of Health, 1997.

Russell, Judy G. The Legal Genealogist. July 16, 2012. https://www.legalgenealogist.com/2012/07/16/of-crime-and-punishment-in-oregon-territory.

Salem Statesman. "'Snake' Led Communal Group through Varying Lifestyles." April 23, 1975.

San Fransisco Call. "Jealous Woman's Freak." September 30, 1895, 3.

———. "Woman With Hands on Face." September 30, 1895.

Seattle Daily Times. "Maud Creffield Anxious to Hang." September 18, 1906, 10.

Seattle Star. "I Got My Man; Am in Jail." May 7, 1906, 1.

State of Oregon. "Our History." https://www.oregon.gov/doc/about/Pages/history.aspx.

State of Oregon v. Dayton Leroy Rogers. S063700, Oregon Supreme Court, March 5, 2021.

State of Oregon v. Scott. 28 Or. 331, 42 P. 1. Oregon Supreme Court, October 28, 1895.

State Rights Democrat. "Circuit Court." December 6, 1895, 1.

———. "The Hannah Case." November 29, 1895, 3.

———. "The Insane Asylum." February 3, 1866, 3.

The Statesman. "Snake Led Communal Group through Varying Lifestlyes." April 23, 1975.

Stauth, Cameron. "Snake Brooks." *One Dollar Magazine* (February 1976): 2–10.

———. "Snake Brooks, Belinda, and the Death of Roy Dirks." *One Dollar Magazine* (February 1976): 19–28.

Thompson, Robert. "Just Science: Identification: Just the Molalla Forest Serial Killer." National Institute of Justice. February 2019. https://www.ojp.gov/ncjrs/virtual-library/abstracts/just-science-identification-just-molalla-forest-serial-killer

U.S. Census. "1850 United States Federal Census for Charity Lamb." White, Missouri, November 18, 1850.

Van Nostrand, Jim. "A Disaster by Which Others Are Measured." *Daily Astorian*, October 12, 2018.

Weather Atlas. "May Weather Forecast and Climate." https://www.weather-atlas.com/en/oregon-usa/oregon-city-weather-may#rainfall.

Weekly Eugene. "Severed Thigh Found in Dumpster." August 20, 2020.

Weekly Oregon Statesman. "Charity Lamb." October 18, 1889, 6.

Wergeland, Kari. "'Micro-History' on Sect Murder Has Seattle Ties." *Seattle Times*, December 7, 2003, K9.

Western Regional Climate Center. "Oregon's Top 10 Weather Events of the 1900s." September 2008. https://wrcc.dri.edu/Climate/extremes_or.php#top3.ss.

Wheeling Register. "A Masked Woman." October 1, 1895, 2.

Wilkes, Charles, and J.H. Young. *Map of the Oregon Territory*. Serman & Smith, 1844.

Withycombe, Claire. "Killer Maintains Innocence." *The Nugget*, June 24, 2015, 6.

World Atlas. "The US States with the Most Serial Killings." April 27, 2017. https://www.worldatlas.com/articles/the-us-states-with-the-most-serial-killings.html.

ABOUT THE AUTHOR

Jennifer Chambers is a writer and podcaster. She writes both fiction and nonfiction. Her podcasts, *The Courage Checklist* and *Writer's Radio*, are available wherever you access podcasts. Her books can be accessed at your favorite bookstore or online. Follow her on Instagram @thecouragechecklist for her latest news, appearances, updates and cat photos.

Visit us at
www.historypress.com
....